A FAMILY'S ENDLESS JOURNEY BETWEEN OAXACA, MEXICO, AND CALIFORNIA

Teresa Figueroa Sánchez

A FAMILY'S ENDLESS JOURNEY BETWEEN OAXACA, MEXICO, AND CALIFORNIA

Fragmented Spaces, Fragmented Identities

The Latinx Studies Collection

Collection Editor

Manuel Callahan

LPp

First published in 2024 by Lived Places Publishing

British Library Cataloguing in Publication Data
A CIP record for this book is available from the British Library

ISBN: 9781916985308 (pbk)
ISBN: 9781916985322 (ePDF)
ISBN: 9781916985315 (ePUB)

Cover design by Fiachra McCarthy
Book design by Rachel Trolove of Twin Trail Design
Typeset by Newgen Publishing UK

Lived Places Publishing
Long Island
New York 11789

www.livedplacespublishing.com

I dedicate this autoethnography to my mother, whose radical love for her children took her to faraway lands for very long seasons. I just hope to do justice to your/my/our stories in love, respect, dignity, and admiration. *Dedico esta autoetnografía a mi mamá cuyo amor radical por sus hijo/as la llevó a tierras lejanas por temporadas muy largas. Solo espero hacerle justicia a su/mis/ nuestras historias con amor, respeto, dignidad, y admiración.*

My two young sons and their partners have been instrumental throughout this journey. Without your love, I would have never been able to transcend myself as a woman living in a foreign country. I thank you for your incredible editing skills, patience, and support.

I am forever grateful to my colleagues Manuel Callahan, Chris McAuley, Veronica Montes, Alicia Re Cruz, and Lorenzo Covarrubias for your intellectual support and friendship through many years. I would have not been able to tell this story without your support.

Abstract

This book discusses the journey from Oaxaca, México, to California, and all of the in-between spaces of community within a context of confrontations with racial patriarchal capitalism that negate my existence as a human being. It focuses on the power of *comunalidad* as it engenders sensibilities, creative practices, and vernacular wisdoms rooted in Putla, Oaxaca, it continues through clashes with neoliberal agribusiness as an immigrant worker in Santa Marta, California, and it converges on the campus of the University of California, *Tres Calmecac*. It argues that *comunalidad* informs how migrants resist neoliberal fragmented identities, and negotiate the forces of racial patriarchal capital from places of origin steeped in *lo común*, across the borderlands, agribusiness, and academe.

Keywords

Comunalidad
Mexican farm workers
Mexican immigration
Decolonial theory
Mexican women
Mexican immigrant education
The US-Mexican border
Racial, patriarchal capital

Contents

Learning objectives

Students will understand major ideas and concepts drawn from decolonial theory in order to analyze the experience of migrant lives in society.

Students will develop the ability to analyze autoethnography as a methodological tool to study major socio-cultural experiences and processes across time and space.

Students will understand the power of *comunalidad* in relation to systems of domination.

Students will learn to map out their *facultad* to foresee social barriers in their professional development.

Trigger warning

This book is based on personal experiences some of which are very painful. Chapters two and four narrate traumatic personal experiences that may trigger post-traumatic reactions. Please be advised.

Introduction

I remember that my father, and his friends, sponsored the feast that brought the community together in the celebration of the carnival event. Because he was a *mayordomo* during the carnival, he purchased three goats to feed dancers and onlookers in the community. In doing this, he complied with his communal obligation, or *cargo*, to share food and drinks with everybody. I felt so happy seeing the carnival dancers wearing their handmade costumes and dancing right in front of my home to honor my father's commitment to the festive event and to the community. I lived in the small town of Putla, in Oaxaca, México, as a child and adolescent where community was present in daily life. Although I eventually moved to México City, and then to California, I drew strength from my sense of self rooted in a community praxis common to Oaxaca and the place I called home.

A Family's Endless Journey weaves ethnography and personal experiences as I reflect on my family's journey as migrants. Upon crossing the United States-Mexican border, I began experiencing racist microaggressions and political rituals of dehumanization; an effort to turn me into an inferior colonized being dwelling in the "zone of nonbeing, [or] an extraordinary sterile and arid region" (Fanon, 1967, p. 10). The systemic racialized attacks worked to strip me of my historical memory while simultaneously turning me into a low-value, dehumanized, neoliberal subject/worker. In the process of writing critically and reflectively as a cultural anthropologist, I found that my sense of *comunalidad* rebuilt my identity, place, belonging, emotions, and collectiveness across multiple spaces that negated my existence as a whole human being. In fact, my sense of self rooted in practical, longstanding *comunalidad* helped me to challenge systemic regimes of racial-patriarchal, and capitalist violence, which I could not escape as a Green Card holder and naturalized citizen, farm worker, worker in the nonprofit world, and university instructor in California. To be sensitive to my native language and culture, I am using words in the Spanish language whose translations can be found in a Glossary at the end of the manuscript.

A Family's Endless Journey attempts to provide a window to reflect on four key moments of my life in a world dominated by the violence of racial-patriarchal capitalism that orders the world using various technologies of exclusion. Chapter one is about growing up in Putla, Oaxaca, rooted in *communalidad* where I had a place and an identity steeped in community, *barrio*, family, and Blue House. I became a communal subject learning the power of cultural identity tied to emotions, resilience, friendship, and sharing as well as political awareness acutely aware of persecution, justice, and anti-imperialist stances of an unjust world. Chapter two examines my grandparents', my parents', and my own painful and emotional experiences crossing the United States-Mexican border and the in-between places that attempted to turn me into an inferior or fragmented racialized/colonized "Other", living in the zone of nonbeing. Chapter three discusses my insertion as a neoliberal farm worker in California's rich agricultural fields, and the fierce fight to survive brutal exploitation in the agro-industry. I examine this experience from the perspective of ethics to show that Mexican migrant laborers find dignity and strength in their living labor to resist the domination of agrarian capital. Chapter four discusses my education or *facultad*, which I built by learning English as a Second Language, attending the public university, and becoming an adjunct professor at the University of California at *Tres Calmecac* (UCTC). Although I was part of Chicana/o historical struggles, the Chicana and Chicano Studies Department and white educational institutions almost destroyed my *facultad*. In short, my deep and extended sense of rootedness, based on *comunalidad*, sustained and nurtured me as I negotiated how racial patriarchal capitalism attempted to racialize me as a migrant, farm worker, nonprofit worker, and adjunct faculty. Pseudonyms are used throughout the book to protect personal identities.

1
Through a child's eyes

I was approximately ten years old when my siblings and I went with a group of friends to *Las Peñitas*, one of the rivers making up the border of our town. It was the day following a heavy rainstorm, but we were unbothered by the increased flow of the river or the warnings from town elders. Suddenly, dozens of snakes erupted from one of the newly fallen trees and began to swarm the river. The older children immediately ran out of the raging waters, but my eight-year-old sister, Margot, did not see the snakes. We desperately screamed at her to come out of the water, but she could not hear us. The snakes swam past her toward the other bank of the river and she was unharmed. That day, I nearly died of *¡susto!* I also learned the power of community and caring for each other in the face of danger. In this chapter, I reflect on my memories of growing up as a child and adolescent living in the small town of Putla, Oaxaca, and my eventual move to México City. I found that my identity was rooted in many Mesoamerican cultural practices, sensibilities, and emotions steeped in a sense of place, and *comunalidad*, that nurtured me as a whole being belonging to a community located in a semi-tropical territory in Oaxaca.

Some Indigenous Oaxaqueño thinkers say that *los pueblos Indígenas* live in *comunalidad*, which they define as a lifestyle and a specific structure of social organization in the community (Maldonado, 2015). Still other Indigenous scholars conceptualize *comunalidad* as a way of life and as a lived experience. In this context, living *comunalidad* is appreciating *saberse naturaleza* (knowing that we are part of the environment), living with respect as part of the world (Martínez Luna, 2022). They insist that *comunalidad* "is not only an epistemic concept, it is also the cultural matrix of Mesoamerican civilizations" (Sánchez-Antonio, 2021, p. 699). Today, scholars who are the children of Indigenous Oaxaqueños generally identify with the *comunalidad* claimed and maintained by their parents, although they live in other parts of the world (Nicolas, 2021). The social reproduction of *comunalidad* exists outside of physical and geographical Indigenous territories found in the state of Oaxaca. The debate about what is or what constitutes *comunalidad* is clearly far from settled. As a child and adolescent living in Putla, Oaxaca, I developed an identity based on Mesoamerican *comunalidad*, or communal praxis, that engendered cultural sensibilities, social commitments, and political awareness.

Community praxis

My Putleca identity is deeply rooted in the *comunalidad*, and in the community I claim, and it includes memories of living in my neighborhood, Blue House, semi-tropical territory, its foodways, markets and pre-Hispanic *tianguis*. In the 1960s, Putla Villa de Guerrero was a relatively small town located in the cradle of Mesoamerican white, red, and blue corn. Putla is enclosed by the breathtaking Sierra Madre mountain range in the southern state of Oaxaca, México. An Indigenous word meaning place of mist, Putla is known for its mantle of heavy mist that hovers over the valley until it dissipates with the sunrise. For some people, Putla is part of the Mixtec region populated by ethnic groups such as the Amuzgos, Tacuates, Mixtecs, and Triqui. For others, Putla belongs to the Costa Chica because of its shared border with the state of Guerrero in the north. According to Grimes (1998), la Mixteca Alta, la Mixteca Baja, and la Mixteca de la Costa converge in the Valley of Putla. Putla is a very important *cabecera de distrito* with juridical responsibilities over small towns, many of which are Indigenous communities with a unique traditional dress, *usos y costumbres*, languages, and dialects. It rains six months of the year, giving Putla a semi-tropical climate. The town is located in a lush valley with four main rivers: *La Cuchara*, Yuteé or *las Peñitas, Copala, y la Purificación*. Putla is located 5 hours away from the state capital of Oaxaca and 12 hours from México City by bus. When I was growing up, Putla was a beautiful, and a small town.

My paternal grandfather purchased a plot of land and he sold to my father, his older son, a portion of his land for a symbolic amount. During the 1950s, my father constructed his adobe house on top of a small hill in a neighborhood known as *barrio de Arroyos*. Many *arrieros* from different regions of the State of Oaxaca settled in this neighborhood. During this time, one or two local *caciques* owned beautiful concrete two-story homes. Like my father, people constructed adobe homes along the perfectly lined up pebble streets that converge in the main marketplace, the church, and the *presidencia municipal*. Putla has the infrastructure of colonial towns in México.

Like many other homes in town, my house has the living room facing the main public street, an interior hallway to place beds, and the kitchen looking at the backyard. For years, my father planted different varieties of mango, avocado, banana, papaya, lemon, and coffee trees in the backyard. He also brought large and small circular and rectangular pebbles from the river to place in the middle of the backyard. There he built a place where clothes would dry under the sun. I loved to lay down on the stones to see the white and black clouds passing through the valley. My mother also planted beautiful red bougainvillea and yellow and pink roses in the home's backyard. My mother loved seeing *chupamirtos*, *palomas*, and butterflies feeding off the plants. On hot days in spring, we sat under the red bougainvillea for respite and to refresh drinking *chilacayote*. One year, the house was painted in blue simply because it was my mother's favorite color. We called it the Blue House. As a child growing up in a small rural town with no more than 1,000 families, the Blue House and the backyard looked similar to others. As an adolescent, I was proud of the *barrio de Arroyos* because it was a beautiful place integrated in the semi-tropical territory.

Because Putla was a small town, I had a very strong sense of belonging and being part of the community. I remember that adults would greet me on the streets. They would say, bye, Guille. Sometimes, women would stop me on the streets to inquire about my mother or father's wellbeing. My affiliation became more complicated as an adolescent because people would also identify each other based on last name. People would ask, *¿hija de quien eres?* Or whose daughter, are you? when they did not recognize me. I would reply, my mother is Guilla. Or they would say, *¿en que barrio vives?* Or, what is your neighborhood? People saw me and I was happy to belong to the *barrio*, and to a respected, loved family. My three younger siblings and I were born and raised in the Blue House while my older siblings were born in rented homes. My mother would always say that we had our belly buttons buried in the patio. My older siblings had their belly button somewhere in Putla. I lived in Putla until I was 16 years old.

Marketplace and *tianguis*

My identity as a Putleca developed in communal experiences such as going to the marketplace and the *tianguis* every day to purchase food. Putla was embedded in an economic web of complex regional marketplaces where people from other regions and towns sold their products. The marketplace was a square block covered with tin sheets located right in the middle of the town, near the Catholic church and the jail. Many women would sell their products in the *tianguis*.

The marketplace had many small stalls where women would sell their merchandise. Some women would sell meat like beef, pork, and chickens while others would specialize in the sale of vegetables like watercress, tomatoes, chilis, and zucchini squash. A few women would sell homemade food in the marketplace. On weekends, people from other towns came to sell their seasonal products in the *tianguis* or in the streets near the marketplace. This was a unique, intercultural space beaming with precolonial traditions of exchange and social life. Markets had their origins in the sixteenth century with the expansion of the Western/modern colonial market; and all places of exchange were "destituted" from vernacular languages (Mignolo, 2021, p. 249). Actually, as the precolonial *tianguis* proves, such places were reconstituted not only as places of exchange of food stuffs, but also as sites of knowledge, and social relations.

I recall that Indigenous women of the *tianguis* would display small quantities of fruit like *granadas*, mangoes, bananas, or small apples. Dressed in their multi-colored *huipiles*, they would sit in the open-market spaces of the *tianguis* to sell seasonal products. Black women from Pinotepa Nacional would also come to sell fresh and dry fish in big handwoven baskets. Peasants from the surrounding towns would arrive at Putla to sell corn, dry chilis, or sugarcane products. *Caña*, *guanavos*, *huajes*, bananas, and sweet ripe mangoes would be placed on a tarp on the floor, and customers would choose which produce they wanted to buy. In the *tianguis*, before paying, people would bargain the final price and the *chiso*. The marketplace and the *tianguis* were filled with sweet aromas of ripe fruit, colorful aromatic yellow mangoes, and red hot chilis. In a decolonial turn, Mignolo says, we must rebuild "communal places exchanges" to include "gnoseological (knowing) and aesthesic (sensing, emotioning, subject-formation)" (2021, pp. 246 and 249).

I loved going to the *tianguis* because my mother would give me extra money to purchase treats for everyone in the family. For example, I would buy two or three pesos of sweet brown yucca, so everybody in the family would eat a little piece. Women from the surrounding villages would sell white salty yucca, or they would bring my favorite sweet brown yucca cooked with sugarcane molasses. The women would wrap the yucca in big leaves from the tropical *buchicata* plant. One day, after I ate the yucca, I decided to lick the big *buchicata* leaf because it still had sweet juices dripping from it. A second after I licked the leaf, my tongue burned like hell! I could not close my mouth until the burning sensation stopped minutes later. When my mom saw me, she said, *eso le pasa a las comelonas* (that happens to gluttons). My mother scolded me for being selfish. She then told me to wash my mouth with clean water from the water tank. Although the water did not erase the burning sensation, it decreased it. At least I could stop dripping saliva and close my mouth. *Buchicata* leaf contains a white liquid containing calcium oxalate that provokes irritation in the mouth, tongue, and lips. I never again licked *buchicatas*. As a child, licking the big green leaves was below the knowing and beyond the sensing of the *tianguis* experience. Despite the tensions, I learned the power of sharing with my family and to think as a member of a collective through foodways.

When I was about 10 years old, I remember going daily to the marketplace to shop for groceries because we did not have electricity and people did not own refrigerators at home. Sometimes, my mother would ask me to buy a specific product in the marketplace. For instance, she would tell me to buy a kilogram of beef steak with her friend *doña* Natalia, a kilo of tomatoes, and a bunch of *papaloquelites* or *pierna de vieja*. I would take my hand-woven palm basket and the money, and I would cheerfully walk on the beautiful cobbled streets to the marketplace. As I walked, I repeated the list for fear of forgetting an essential item. Un kilo de bistec, un kilo de tomatoes. Perhaps because we were poor, our Putleca diet was very healthy since we ate meat two times per week and consumed edible plants the rest of the week.

Once in a while, my mom would give me money to buy my favorite snacks in the marketplace and I felt very special. I would buy my favorite *gelatina de pata*, which I would eat right in the marketplace. Because I did not want to share my treat with my siblings, I would eat it before returning home with the groceries. At other times, I would buy one stick of sugarcane for myself or I would buy several sticks for all of the family. I learned that peasants from the surrounding villages would bring two kinds of sugarcane sticks. One was soft and the other was really hard. The soft variety was called white sugarcane, and it was more expensive. I would peel the soft sugarcane with my teeth and eat it before coming back home. Other times I would secretly peel the hard kind of sugarcane with my father's *machete* at home. Sometimes, I did not want to share the sugarcane with my siblings, nor did I want to wait to eat it. My mother would scold me for not sharing snacks with my siblings. I loved going to the marketplace because my mom would always give me extra money to buy my favorite treat or sweet cassava. I always had to be careful of not coming home with leftovers or additional evidence, so I would throw the wrapper on the street so as to not give myself away. Unlike rational capitalist consumers engaged in the exchange of merchandise and money, I participated in an emotional experience of feeling special, seeing colorful delicious fruits, smelling sweet aromas of food, and hearing simultaneous conversations in various languages.

I had two Indigenous *nanas*, *doña* Sole and *doña* Estrella, who played an important role developing my communal worldview. They lived with us in the Blue House and I recalled that they were tender, loving, and caring with me and my siblings. In the absence of my migrant mother, they would send me to the marketplace to buy groceries and they would give me the shopping list. They would say buy meat, bread, or milk, and I had to decide how much meat or milk to buy. Sometimes, our neighbors would see me with the container in hand and would tell me not to buy milk. My neighbor, or women in the community who watched for each other, would say that so-and-so added water to the milk and it was not good for drinking. A few greedy men would put our health at risk for a few pesos by adding water to milk, but consumers would immediately notice the watery taste of milk and spread the word. Word-of-mouth information was a way of taking care of each other in the community.

On Saturday or Sunday when the marketplace was full of people from all over the Costa Chica and the Mixtec regions, people would buy the famous *masa de chivo*. This was made up of ground corn, chili, tomatoes, avocado leaves, and goat meat. This would be cooked in an underground oven until flavorful and tender. Given the difficulty of cooking it, many women just purchased it from *doña* María because she cooked the best *masa de chivo* in all of the town. Street vendors, women sellers in the *tianguis*, and local families like my own loved eating *masa de chivo*. Although the state of Oaxaca is internationally known for its *moles*, I ate *mole* at special celebrations like weddings. Banana leaf *tamales*, *pozole*, and *mole* were not an everyday food, but *masa de chivo* was a staple food of the local cuisine.

Another favorite shopping activity was related to buying *semitas*, *pan de llema*, or *pan de muerto* at the baker's home. Every evening, I would take my basket to buy ten pesos of bread. As I walked back home, I carried my basket full of freshly baked round *semitas* sprinkled with sesame seeds. As I passed by *doña* Tomasa's home in the *barrio de Arroyos*, her big black dog would try to steal a piece of bread from my basket. I would feel the sudden weight of the dog's paw on my basket, in an effort to knock some of the bread out. Frequently, the dog would sneak behind me and grab a piece of bread. Sometimes, I saw the dog approaching me and I would just whisper, *¡perro!* At other times, I would stomp my foot and yell at the dog. I tried to scare him away, but it was a big, black, scary dog.

The dog would prey on anyone walking by *doña* Tomasa's home. My sisters, like other women in our neighborhood, would also deal with the badly behaved dog. When my mother was at home, my younger sister Margot would be sent to sell gelatins. One day, she was walking with her basket full of treats when the dog sneaked behind her. It managed to take one gelatin, although my sister resisted him. Because the dog was very big, she fell, scratching her legs. My sister came home crying, with her knees bleeding. When my mom asked her what happened, she explained that the dog had taken some gelatins with him. I do not know why mother never went to discuss the issue with the elderly *doña* Tomasa. My sisters and I still remember the scary black dog and laugh.

I also remember that my mother or older siblings sent me to the market or the *tianguis* to buy comic books. As a child, I was an avid reader of *revistas de historietas*, which would arrive in Putla once per week. I remember that I would run to the store to purchase our favorite ones. My siblings and I read *Kalimán*, the white blue-eyed Middle Eastern superhero wearing a white turban, a comic storybook where he fights evil. Kalimán and his friend Solin fought together, but Kalimán would always preach "patience, much patience". We also read *Memín Pinguín* . Memin was a young Black boy who lived in the city. He was a little rascal whose mother worked as a domestic employee for a wealthy family. On the weeks we could not buy the books we would rent them in the parks, near the *tianguis*, magazine and newspaper stalls. Sometimes, we would borrow them from a friend, but had to return them on time or they would stop lending us them. My siblings and I would take turns, from oldest to youngest, to read the many racist and stereotypical comic story books that we purchased.

As an adolescent, my favorite story books were western novels, which were very popular in Putla. I would sit to read the story book by candlelight at night. Most of my male friends purchased *Estefanía*, the story of a cowboy who would travel from Kansas City, in the United States, to the open and wild western frontier. Estefanía always killed Native Americans who opposed the marching of cattle ranching herds and colonial settlement on Native American lands. My older siblings would ask me to buy an issue, which we would trade after reading it. Popular comic books and western novels circulated among Putlecos who were symbolically learning the politics of settler colonialism.

I further recall that a red plane flew over Putla once or twice per year dropping flyers and very small bottles of Coca-Cola. Usually, the airplane would fly low to avoid the wind carrying these into the mango trees. Then, hundreds of little bottles containing a black sweet liquid fell one by one to the cheering of children going crazy on the streets. I would stand in the middle of the street and look up at the gifts falling from the sky. All the children in town would stop doing their chores and run towards the street to catch the bottles before they hit the ground. After the airplane left, kids tried to open the bottles by twisting the tiny caps. Others tried to open the bottles by using their teeth to remove the caps. The Coca-Cola bottles were hermetically closed, so we would usually fail in the endeavor. Only older and smarter, or stupid, kids, could open the bottle with their teeth. Frustrated young children who could not drink the beverage would smash the tiny bottle with a stone. Other people would put the bottles on the Virgen de Guadalupe's altar or on the countertop of a small grocery store. There, the tiny bottle of Coca-Cola would be displayed for everyone to see. I imagine that Coca-Cola corporation flew its airplanes all over the region to promote the consumption of its soft beverage since these were still untapped capitalist consuming markets.

Cultural sensibilities

The *comunalidad*, I learned while I lived in Putla, includes many cultural practices that continue to shape my identity as a Putleca. As a child and young woman, I lived in *comunalidad* for the first 16 years of my life when I participated in many cultural fiestas like *la calenda* and the carnival learning the power of communal obligation, sharing, affection, and spirituality.

The Catholic church priest organized *la calenda*, an annual parade to honor *la Virgen de Natividad*, on September 6 and 8. Young *madrinas* would parade through the neighborhoods. The *madrinas* would carry homemade papier mâché flowers, while local musicians led the parade. Usually, each *madrina* would invite several companions to bring flower bouquets to the virgin's altar. At 5 a.m. the musical band would start the parade in the church and from there it would go to each *barrio*, stopping in the house of every *madrina*. After all the *madrinas* were gathered, we would go to the church to hear Mass. Then, we would make the flower offerings to the Virgin. After Mass, the musicians would walk towards each *barrio* to return to the *madrina*'s home. We would all eat *mole* and drink *agua fresca*. To celebrate *la Virgen de Natividad*, we would usually prepare months ahead of time. When I was about eight years old, in 1969, I participated in the town's most famous Catholic fiesta.

All the *madrinas* and companions would wear new dresses that the local seamstress would make months ahead. I remember that my sister Maribel, who was a few years older than me, came back to town from México City. She sewed me a purple suit with white flowers using the latest *terlenka*, a typical hippy fabric. I felt so elegant wearing my new suit. My mom purchased a pair of shoes for me to wear during the parade, for not a single *madrina* or companion walked barefoot during the parade. They were white and matched very nicely with my suit. The shoe size was exactly what I needed. The shoes were beautiful. However, the shoes had a two-inch heel, which I did not like at all. I could not walk wearing high heels on the streets that were woven with irregular pebbles from the local rivers.

One day, I decided to take my shoes to the shoemaker who had his repair shop close to the marketplace. I walked from my house for about ten minutes carrying my white shoes in a plastic bag. When I arrived at the shoemaker's store, I entered without hesitation. I stood on my toes, and I placed the white shoes on the counter. I asked him to cut the heel in half. He took the shoes and examined them. I could barely make out the top of his counter, so he was peering over the counter to get a look at me. He stopped working on a shoe and, then, asked me, "are you sure that you want the heels to be cut in half?" I replied "yes" without a doubt. He said, "It will cost you five *pesos*. Come back in a week." A week later, I came back to pick up my shoes. I was so happy. I now had the perfect shoes. I felt like a city girl, just like my cousins when they came to visit us from México City. They were always well dressed and wore nice shoes on. The day before the parade, I tried my shoes on. My feet felt weird. I looked down on my feet and saw my pointed shoes. I was stunned at the weird shape of my shoes. Upon examination, I noticed that the heel was lower than the front of the shoes. I thought the shoemaker had destroyed my beautiful white shoes. I felt tears rolling down on my round cheeks. We were very poor, and I could not ask for a new pair of shoes.

On the day of the parade, I woke to the rooster singing at dawn. I took a warm shower, careful to not destroy my curly hair. I put on my new *terlenka* suit, earrings, socks, and my newly pointed shoes. As I excitedly walked to my friend's house carrying a bouquet of flowers, I could hear the musical band coming closer and closer. I ran carefully in my crooked shoes, fearing I would be left behind. After I arrived at my friend's home, the musical group came in to pick us up in the *barrio de Arroyos*. The *madrina* led the small and very tight group that followed the musicians. House after house, we picked up the *madrinas* to go to Mass and then brought them back to their houses afterwards. We arrived at Chela's house in the *barrio de la Cureña* because her daughter, Rocio, was a *madrina*. They lived in an adobe house with an enclosed front yard. When the *madrinas*, companions, and the entire *comparsa* entered the front yard, we all followed them inside the front yard.

I stood next to the blooming roses near the *corral*. Because there were so many people in the parade, someone pushed me against the *corral*. I easily lost my balance because I was wearing my pointed shoes. So, I took a step back to avoid falling into the *corral* and thorny rose plants. Suddenly, I heard a puffing sound. Surprised, I turned my head and I saw my white pointed shoes painted with blood. I lifted my shoe up and looked once more. I had stepped on a *¡pollito!* When I saw the baby chick intestines on the floor, I was stunned in horror. I could not move, nor could I speak. I was terrified at the scene. My heart, hands, and legs were shaking. My only thought was to flee before Chela saw her dead *pollito*. I could not face Chela's angry words, nor did I have money to pay for a dead chick. Because the *comparsa* was playing religious music, the social environment was festive. I could see *la madrina* smiling while she was distributing delicious food. I felt that *la Virgen de Natividad* was not happy with the death of the baby chick. As a child, I was very scared of having killed the baby chick, even though it was an accident.

As I was fleeing the scene, I was thinking of my mother's chickens and pigs and how she would enlist my help for their care. Usually, my mother would tell me to feed the chickens in the morning and I would take a container with dry corn to scatter for them. I would then wash and refill a container with clean water. Then, I remember that I was about eight years old when my mother asked me to kill a chicken. I had seen how she killed and cooked the chickens, but I had never killed one. I was terrified and I did not want to do it.

I took the chicken with my hands and held it upside down. I do not know exactly how long I stood there without saying anything. I remember feeling angry at my mother while the chicken sang and flapped its wings. My strong-willed mother insisted that I needed to kill the animal. I remember thinking, *¡qué mujer tan necia!* (what a stubborn woman). Finally, I grabbed its legs with one hand and the neck with the other. I stood there crying. In a moment of valor, I pulled the neck away, but it did not die. I did not kill the chicken. It started to flap its wings. My mother then screamed at me, *¡matala que la estas haciendo sufrir!* (kill it because you are making it suffer). I sheepishly responded, *¡no puedo!* (I can't) and I stomped my right foot on the floor. My mother, who was washing clothes, came running like a gazelle and killed the chicken. That sad day, I did not eat chicken for dinner. Although I was a child, I was old enough to kill a chicken. This was a traumatic and cruel event such that I never forgot. As a girl, my mother was teaching me to become a traditional home maker raising, killing, and cooking domestic animals.

The carnival

As a child, I participated in the carnival celebration, but I did not partake too much in the religious side of the event. As in many towns in Oaxaca, the carnival is a religious celebration that builds solidarity, respect, collaboration, and belonging in the community. Of all the cultural events in Putla, the carnival defined my lifetime identity as a Putleca. I remember the annual carnival celebration took place during the week of Lent.

To participate in the carnival, men made their *los viejos* costumes by cutting and stitching hundreds of multicolored stripes into old pants and a long sleeve shirt. The costume is called *tilichis*. In addition, *viejos* wore a mask so they would not be recognized. They also put on a big handmade palm hat characteristic of the *los viejos* event. There was no carnival without two or three handcrafted *toritos*, and *cunis* costumes. *Los viejos* also carried with them eggshells filled with confetti during the fiesta celebration. They would dance throughout the town, stopping in each neighborhood, and onlookers would follow them all day long. The *mayordomos* would feed *masa de chivo* and *tepache* to dancers who came to honor the sponsors. The carnival also had a queen who accompanied the dancers all day long.

The carnival was an intense festive event where people in the community entered into a liminal space of transgression. Men would traditionally dress in their costumes and gather in the town's main plaza. Usually, all *viejos* would dance up and down to the tune of the town's clarinet and drum players from the local *comparsa* group. One dancer would lift *el torito* above his head, dancing in circles with it. As he danced, he would purposely or accidentally hit anyone next to him. All dancers would try to avoid being hit with *el torito* because they could fall at the feet of other dancers. One or two men would dress as a *cunis* and would carry a stick with a nail on the end. With the stick, they would hit people in the head. Boys would dare each other to touch them, but would risk being hit on the head with the nail. Once in a while, a woman looking at the dancers would be hit on the head. Dancers and onlookers had to always be on the lookout to avoid being hit on the head. At this point, the transgression of being hit with the nail on the head was generally not a personal attack. *El torito* and the *cuni* would make the carnival a happy, communal celebration which was exciting to watch from a safe distance. *Los viejos* would also take empty eggshells filled with confetti and crush them on people's heads. Sometimes, a *viejo* would take real eggs and crush them on a young woman's head. She would be annoyed at having to go home to clean. During the week of Lent, all the *viejos* would dance, eat, and drink *tepache* all day to the tune of the town's musical group. As an adolescent living in Putla, I loved the carnival because it gave me a sense of belonging in the territory.

There was also another group of dancers called *las mascaritas*. Some dancers would wear a female or male costume. *Las mascaritas* were composed of a group of ten men, all of whom practiced the dance for months. It was a very structured dance and its own rhythm. Unlike *los viejos*, all the men would form two lines and each had a specific place. They would face each other and dance towards the middle. Then, they would go around each other and return to the starting line without turning their backs. Like *los viejos*, *las mascaritas* would eat and dance for hours to the tune of a *comparsa*, parading through the neighborhoods of the town. In this dance, some men would dress in female costumes, challenging patriarchal heteronormative and gender roles.

When I was an adolescent, my father was part of the group of men who were *mayordomos* for each carnival. My mother remembers that he volunteered along with his *compadre* and a friend from the *barrio de Arroyos*. Each one of them had to sponsor the food to feed the *viejos*, *las mascaritas*, and the onlookers. In exchange, *mayordomos* were highly esteemed and respected for their generosity. The *cargo* system was an institution developed by Indigenous communities that involved social, economic, religious, and political obligations and responsibilities of every member of the community. Eric Wolf (1957) considered the *mayordomia* as a cultural and religious institution or a mechanism of social prestige and economic reciprocity. In Putla, many *mayordomos* used their own resources or acquired large debts in sponsoring the communal celebration, and in doing so, they became respectful members. Jaime Martínez Luna (2010) explains that the *cargo* system is a model of democratic organization where elected individuals govern the community. When I asked my mother about this event, she could not remember details of my father's expenses, or how he was selected for this important service in the community.

I remember that my father purchased three goats for the carnival celebration. A few days before the main celebration, my father brought the goats to our house and tied them to a mango tree. He also went to the river and carefully selected stones. These stones were for the underground pit, so he carefully selected them to not overheat in the oven-pit. The night before the celebration, several of his friends came down to kill the goats and to cook the *masa de chivo*. I just remember the goats bleating with a high pitch full of terror. I was too afraid to watch how the men were killing and cleaning the goat meat. The butchers placed the meat in big *cazuelas de barro* and the women cooked it.

My mother and other women prepared the food and the drinks for the celebration when my father was a *mayordomo*. I remember that she purchased, or borrowed from other women, several big, really big, *ollas de barro* since she had to feed the entire town. To make the *tepache* for the celebration, she bought big quantities of pineapples, corn, and chilis. She carefully roasted them.

Once she mixed these ingredients, she placed them in two pots. She would then add water and kilograms of hard sugarcane. The *tepache* had to ferment in big pots that were placed in the darkest corner of the Blue House for months. Once in a while, she tasted it and added hard sugarcane, so it would ferment correctly. This had to be carefully done because *tepache tierno* (inadequate fermentation) would cause diarrhea. A few days before the carnival, my mom would roast and grind more chilis. After this was ready, she added these to the pot. *Tepache* was a delicious sweet, sour, hot, and very refreshing homemade alcoholic drink. *Los viejos* and *las mascaritas* would drink *tepache* to get the energy to dance intensively for hours. Of course, they also got drunk. Under the watchful eye of the adults, I drank a little bit of *tepache*, but did not get drunk. Well, just felt a little dizzy.

My mother and her friends would also cook *masa de chivo* to feed everybody in the community. She bought one big *cazuela de barro* and borrowed a few more from her friends. These were big clay pots into which she put ground corn, chilis, salt, and avocado leaves. Then, the women would add the meat in the *cazuelas* and mix all the ingredients. Afterwards, men would place them carefully inside the fire pit, covering it with banana leaves and soil. The meat would remain in the oven under the watchful eye of men who were chatting and drinking around the oven-pit for hours. That is, they stood guard. When they finally dug out the pots, they placed them on the ground. Although children did not take active part in cooking, they would run around playing all the time. The nights leading to the main celebration were festive, and I greatly enjoyed participating in the event.

On the day of the celebration, I remember that *los viejos* were in the Blue House dancing for hours, celebrating my generous father who was feeding the town their favorite food. I saw women serving *masa de chivo* and *tepache* to the people dancing or watching *los viejos* on the street. When dancers stopped dancing, they sat on the floor to rest. I remember feeling so proud seeing *los viejos* dancing in front of the Blue House. While I watched them dance, I felt the sound of the clarinet and the drum in my blood! I felt so proud that my generous father did not mind feeding the entire town. My mother worked for months to make the event a memorable one. As a young woman, I did not think about patriarchal relations in my household, I just felt proud of my parents.

I remember that the carnival was a rather masculine event since only men dressed in *los viejos* costumes. The fun part was to find out who was who during the dance. This was very difficult since all men wore the same costume. My friends and I loved watching the *viejos*. Sometimes, I would say to my friend, "That one is Victor" pointing my finger to a dancer in the crowd. She would reply, "*No, pendeja* (no, jerk). That is Roberto, the son of Juan." One would only identify someone if they spoke to you. There were times when we did not recognize anyone. As a child and adolescent, I did not wonder whether the carnival or *los viejos* were pre-Hispanic or colonial cultural traditions.

Today, *los viejos* is a very famous popular fiesta that the State of Oaxaca promotes, but it has changed drastically because women dance in *los viejos* and carry the *torito* too. People now wear costumes that resemble lizards and dinosaurs. Nonetheless, hundreds of tourists arrived in Putla to watch or participate in the carnival.

Affection

I played numerous games with my siblings and friends to develop family bonds, and social collaboration, which created a sense of *comunalidad*. A popular game among children and adolescents was to play marbles, so I always played my favorite game with marbles. Although I had three older and three younger siblings, I enjoyed playing marbles with my oldest brother Alfredo. Unlike me, he lived in México City with my paternal grandparents and my aunts and uncles. As a teen, my brother would frequently visit us during his vacation breaks from school. When he came home, I would challenge him to play marbles underneath the big mango trees that my grandfather and my father had planted in the backyard.

I loved playing marbles after tropical storms when the soil still smelled fresh. On the wet ground, I would draw a triangle, and we would place one marble on each corner and one in the center. From a meter away, we would take turns throwing a marble to hit one of the marbles in the triangle. Whoever hit three marbles would win the game. Sometimes, we would bet 10 or 25 cents, and the winner would take the money. I always won. I thought that my left-handed brother was a city boy who did not have enough practice playing marbles. I, on the other hand, played marbles with the boys in the neighborhoods because my migrant mother was not at home. I was very skilled, so much so that I had a little bag full of big and small multi-colored marbles. I never risked losing my favorite marble which was a multicolored big marble. I would cry when my brothers took my favorite marble, or I would fight with them until they returned it. I always bet small marbles with my neighbors while I bet money with my brother. I was not sure if my older brother was a bad player, or if he would just lose on purpose. Many times, I felt that he would let me win the game, but I never asked him. I felt stronger and smarter than my oldest brother. As a girl, I broke gender rules in the *barrio*.

I had a small piggy bank made up from an empty tuna fish can to deposit my not so hard-won money. After the games, I did not want to spend my money, so I would bury the tin can in the backyard. I was always careful not to be seen by my siblings. I always felt that they would take my money away. Any time when I had a little bit of money, I would dig out the tin can. I would drop my coin and quickly bury it again. Most of the time, I buried the piggy bank in the same spot, but sometimes, I would forget to mark the spot. Then, I would spend hours searching for the tin can and I would cry upon failing to find it. At other times, I would forget all about the tin can. I didn't really need money, so I would easily forget about it.

Games immersed me into a world that included nature. When I was about nine years old, I was playing with my older sister Maribel in the backyard where there were several mango trees forming a big green canopy. We climbed on the one bearing the most delicious round mangoes in the whole Costa Chica region. My sister sat on a tall branch and dropped her head down with her legs clamped on the branch. She swung her head up and down while playfully screaming *¡auxilio, auxilio!*

I was standing on the ground laughing, watching her swing from side to side. I saw her long black hair flying like a bird's feathers and I laughed at her fake calls for help. Suddenly, I saw my mother coming out from the Blue House running towards the mango tree screaming, "Maribel, are you okay?" I recall that she looked like a tall pale ghost, thinking that her daughter was in grave danger or that she had fallen from the majestic mango tree. Upon hearing my mom's terrified scream, my sister's body stopped swinging. She sheepishly answered my mother and came down from the tree faster than a monkey. Needless to say, my mom realized that we were playing and she became very angry at us. I was ordered to wash a pile of dirty dishes, while my sister had to sweep the house.

Like other Putleca teenagers, I remember my siblings and our friends in the *barrio de Arroyos* spending hours swimming in the rivers, playing with toads' eggs, and eating on the beach. Several rivers pass by our town, but our favorite was called *"Peñitas"*, located in the northern part of the valley. It would take us an hour of walking to get there.

I was about 12 years old when we were getting ready to go to the river. My aunt, who was walking by our house, told us not to go. "It is dangerous", she said to us. The night before a semi-tropical storm with thunder and lightning fell on the valley and the water was dark brown. It was either a *sábado de gloria* (Holy Saturday) or a saint day. Of course, we did not heed my aunt's advice and left for the river. When we got to the river, the water was indeed brown from the erosion caused by the rain. My siblings and our friends did not care about the color of the water and began swimming in the raging river. A tree with long branches and green foliage was on the edge of the river. A big boulder (hence the name *Peñitas*) was located on the river edge. We would go up the boulder and jump, falling on the deepest side of the river. For hours, we ran, played, jumped, and swam!

We would only rest to eat *totopos con frijol y queso* and we would all sit down to share our food with our friends. Boys would flirt with the young women by playing the guitar. I remember José Feliciano's song *"pueblo mio que estas en la colina"* (my town located on the hill) that a friend sang by the river. They would also sing *Un poco más*, written by our very own famous Putleco songwriter, Alvaro Carrillo. After eating and singing, we would return to swim in the river. It was always fun to go to the river with my friends or my family.

We were cheerfully swimming and playing in the water when snakes suddenly started to climb down from the tree branches. There were hundreds of snakes in heat. When I saw the snakes, I started to scream and ran out of the water. In fact, almost everybody ran out of the water, except my younger sister, Margot, who was about eight years old. My little sister was still in the water and the snakes were swimming on top of her trying to cross the other side of the river. All of us were screaming at her, "Margot, Margot! Come out of the water", but she did not hear us. I was jumping up and down screaming her name, but she did not react. She was either not scared or deaf. *¡Que susto!* The snakes rapidly crossed the river, and my sister did not know about it. When she came out of the water, we told her. She could not believe it. My sister was very strong and not easily frightened. I thought that something was wrong with her, how could she not be scared of the snakes? The older children decided that it was no longer safe, so we took our belongings and went home in a hurry. No one wanted to admit my aunt's warning was right.

Spirituality

Because I had a *nana* who was an Indigenous *curandera*, I believed in the power of the spiritual world. I remember that my *nana*, *doña* Estrella, performed cleansing to cure people from *susto*. When a person experienced extreme fright, the soul would leave the body. A ritual would then be performed to reinstate the soul in the body. *Doña* Estrella, who lived in the Blue House, had an altar with various saints and candles. The healing ceremony would start with rubbing alcohol on a bunch of medicinal herbs that she collected in the forest. She would take an egg and sweep one's body from head to toe with it. She would then crack it open in a water container. She would then read the egg. Then, she would take a sip of *aguardiente* from the bottle and would then spray it on the floor and person while chanting a prayer. I remember that I was always sick of *susto*. Many times, she would cure me in our home, but it depended on the type and intensity of *el susto*. Sometimes, she would take me to the place where I had experienced *el susto*.

On the day when we saw the snakes on the river, *doña* Estrella cured me of *susto*. I recall that I stood in front of her altar with my eyes closed to prevent *aguardiente* from entering my eyes. She rubbed my body with herbs and the egg. Then, she read the egg and diagnosed a strong *susto* with snakes requiring a trip to the river. We walked to *las Peñitas* river, and we stood on the edge of the beach for a few seconds. She gathered branches from the bushes and nearby trees, and she started to call my name saying,

¡Guille, regresa! (Guille, come back). *Doña* Estrella was totally convinced that my soul had left my body and she was calling it back. A few minutes later, we started to walk back home, she walked behind me and whipped the floor with the branches. As I kept walking, she kept calling my name, and whipping the floor, *¡Guille, regresa!* Some games were dangerous as we risked losing our soul. Only the power of the cleansing ritual could unite the physical body with the spiritual one. My *nana* always took care of me and I remember her fondly to this day because she was a powerful influence in my life when my mother was not at home. My *nana* was instrumental in my sense of being as a whole person.

On the steps of my neighbor's home, I remember sitting down with other kids in the *barrio de Arroyos* to listen to stories from older people. Storytelling, as an alternative non-Western epistemology, was a very powerful tool to educate kids in Putla. My mother's stepfather, *el abuelo*, would tell us powerful stories when he visited our small, hilly town located in la Costa Chica de Oaxaca. He would tell us many of his heroic encounters with near death.

One time, he said that he was walking in the middle of the night in the forest by himself. As he was reaching the nearby river, he saw a young woman with long, dark hair and wearing a white dress. The hallowed woman did not speak to him, she just stared. The strong cold wind was bending the branches of the nearby trees, the chill penetrated his bones, and he felt his skin getting *chinita, chinita, chinita* (goosebumps) out of fear. He could not speak, nor could he walk. With great effort, he continued walking towards the river, but his shoulders were heavy. After he took his boots off to cross the river barefoot, he stood for a second on the edge to see the clear blue water. His heart beating like an uncontrolled horse. Despite his fear, he started to cross the river. When he reached the other side of the river, he felt the weight lift from his shoulders. Of the grandchildren listening to his story, I asked him, who was that, *abuelo*? "*Ay, hija*" (my dear), he said looking at me, it was death. "*¡Me libré!*" (I escaped it), he concluded. Death did not distinguish rich or poor, old or young, men or women. Stories of death taught me the power of equality as we were all subject to die one day.

Storytelling also included memories of unfairness and gender relations in a hierarchical town. For example, my mother also told me her story about how my grandmother forgot where she hid her hard-earned coin. As a single poor woman supporting her daughter and an adopted son, a coin was a lot of money. Because Putla did not have banks, most people kept the money at home. Poor people like my grandmother hid the money in small crevices in the adobe walls of their homes.

My mother said that one day my grandmother lost a *peso* that she had hidden in the walls of the adobe kitchen. My grandmother accused my mom of stealing the money, even though she fiercely denied having taken the money. However, my grandmother got really angry and spanked her! Days later, after a big semi-tropical storm with thunder and lightning, my mom found the money right next to the drainage pipe. She could not believe her luck. She took the money and ran as fast as possible to her mother. Holding the money in her right hand, she told her mother, cheerfully with a little bit of irony in her voice, "Look what I found", showing her the coin. My grandmother took the money and did not say a thing. Storytelling created a sense of community, showed the interconnection between the physical and spiritual world, as well as gender and age hierarchies. My identity as a Putleca, a human being, was rooted in many cultural practices and beliefs.

Political awareness

When I was seven years old, more or less, I learned about the political power of the Mexican state and its secret capacity for repression. In Putla, we did not have televisions or electricity to hear the national or international news. However, everybody had a portable radio and we heard many stations from México City. Sometimes, La Sierra Madre mountains would block the signal on cloudy days and we would not have any news. At other times, we would not have money to buy expensive batteries. Even poor people who owned a radio would play it almost all day.

In the Blue House, we had a portable black radio powered with batteries that was placed on a small shelf next to a mirror in the main room. Presidents Gustavo Díaz Ordaz (1964–1970) and Luis Echeverria Álvarez (1970–1976) ordered the arrest, kidnapping, and assassination of hundreds of students, civilians, and dissidents. This event is known as the 1968 Tlatelolco massacre in México City. In this political period, Genaro Vasquez and Lucio Cabañas rose up against the government in the state of Guerrero, México.

El abuelo, as we called him, became a soldier in the state police. He then worked his way up in the armed forces until he became *comandante* in the state of Oaxaca. I remember an October afternoon, the sky was covered with red clouds, when *el abuelo* arrived in town with his entire cavalry. I was afraid to see so many armed men. They tied their horses on the mango trees in the Blue House's backyard and we fetched them water from the tank. The soldiers lay on the floor resting in my backyard, their blue uniforms strewn across the yard. I was afraid to see so many horses neighing, puffing, and stomping their feet on the ground. *El abuelo* explained that they had been chasing a "bad man" named Lucio Cabañas.

Lucio Cabañas had fled the state of Guerrero where he was wanted for rising up against the Mexican government. Cabañas and his men crossed the Sierra Madre mountain range descending into Oaxaca. After chasing Cabañas for several weeks in the mountains, *el abuelo* suspected that he came to Putla to rest with his extremely tired and hungry *guerrilleros*. My step-grandfather, who was in his forties, whispered to me that Lucio Cabañas was in the neighborhood. Then, he showed me a picture asking me if I had seen him in town. Of course, I did not recognize Cabañas. I had not seen the most famous teacher, Lucio Cabañas, turn *guerrillero* in México. My step-grandfather came to my home in the late afternoon because he did not want people to know about his order to chase Cabañas. Before the rooster sang at dawn, *el abuelo* and his cavalry secretly left to continue the political persecution of Lucio Cabañas in Oaxaca.

The State police in Oaxaca kept Lucio Cabañas at bay so he would stay in Guerrero where the police could easily kill him. In 1974, Lucio Cabañas was unjustly assassinated in a confrontation with the police in Tecpan de Galeana, Guerrero. Later, famous Mexican singer Óscar Chávez, among many other singers, sang a *corrido* in honor of Lucio Cabañas:

… En la sierra guerrerense se escribió una gran hazaña,
siete años y cinco meses combatió Lucio Cabañas
protegido por los montes,
brazo armado fue del pueblo, combatiendo por los pobres.
El Zapata de estos tiempos, con su rifle guerrillero
disparaba en las montañas,
combatiendo el mal gobierno con su razón y su arma./

(… In the Guerrerense Sierra a bad deed was written, for seven years and five months fought Lucio Cabañas protected by the forest, armed by the people, fighting for the poor. El Zapata of this time, with his guerrilla pistol shot in the mountains, combating the bad government with his pistol and his reason.)

Years later, my step-grandfather told many stories of how he chased many "bad men" in México. Along la Costa Chica, killers and thieves would be hung from trees. He believed that México was secure by keeping bad men off the streets and out of the State of Oaxaca. As a *comandante* working for the Mexican State, *el abuelo*, who was a sweet step-grandfather, never questioned the secret dirty war or repressive policies of his superiors. Seeing my step-grandfather with his cavalry in my house left a huge interest in politics. The personal became political.

Teachers Antonio and Héctor

Putla had one elementary school named in honor of nineteenth-century President Benito Juárez who was from Guelatao, Oaxaca. I attended this elementary school for six years. In sixth grade, I had a teacher named Antonio whose sexuality turned him into an inferior Other. I loved my teacher Antonio because I developed an awareness of the forces of oppression based on gender and sexuality in the homeplace. The official school not only incorporated me as a member of the nation-state with its official history, but Antonio taught me a sense of social justice and freedom, using a pedagogy of freedom, through extra-curricular activities.

Antonio had a heart for classical poetry. From his class, he would select his best students to learn a poem which would be declared on a special celebration. He selected me to recite a poem on Mother's Day, when the school celebrated all the mothers in town. In preparation I would recite the poem daily with the teacher until I memorized the entire poem. Some of the popular poems were *Reir llorando* by Juan de Dios Peza, and *El brindis del bohemio*. *El brindis del bohemio* had many stanzas, yet I remember one saying:

> *Brindo porque mis versos cuál*
> *saetas lleguen hasta las grietas formadas de metal y granito*
> *del corazón de la mujer ingrata que a desdénes me mata!*

(A toast for my verses like an arrow reach the crevices formed on metal and granite of the ingrate woman's heart whose disdain kills me!)

On Mother's Day, May 10, I dressed up and came to school ready to recite my poem. The day before the celebration, students would place a stage in the center of the basketball court and chairs around for mothers to sit while students recited their poems. When my name was called on the loudspeaker, I walked to the main stage. I was very nervous. I remember that my skinny legs were shaking with every step!

I stood in front of the crowd and I began to recite "... *Querida madre, cuando te pregunten, ¿por qué lloras? Tú contestaras es el que el humo está muy fuerte y me hace llorar"* (Dear mother, when you are asked, why are you crying? you will reply, smoke makes me cry). Suddenly, I went blank! No, no, I said in the middle of the poem. Then, I repeated, "… *Querida madre, cuando te pregunten, ¿por qué lloras?"* I said "¡No, no, no!" in the microphone, shocking everyone. I could not remember the poem. I froze! For the life of me, I could not remember the poem that I had so diligently practiced the prior month.

Teacher Antonio, who was standing nearby, whispered, *Guille, vente* (come back, Guille) while signaling with his hand to walk away from the stage. I stood there for a few minutes trying to remember the poem, and I could not remember it. Teacher Antonio called my name several times, and I finally walked away from the center stage. I felt tears rolling down my cheeks. I was so embarrassed for having forgotten the poem. Neither my mother nor my nannies were there to see me cry! The next day at school, nobody said anything, not a single soul laughed at me.

This incident did not discourage Antonio's love for teaching revolutionary songs to his students. I also recall the *corrido* in honor of Genaro Vásquez. *"Compañero Vásquez Rojas, el fusil que tu dejaste ya lo tengo en la mano"* (Comrade Vásquez Rojas, the pistol that you left behind, I already have it in my hand). I remember my teacher with tender love for not shaming me or excluding me for having a memory lapse in public. Antonio was my first revolutionary teacher who taught me about injustices and compassion.

Putla's secondary school was also named after famous nineteenth-century anarchist Ricardo Flores Magón. I attended secondary school for three years. The school had a vocational orientation in agrarian studies, so I learned to take care of chickens, rabbits, and bees. I loved feeding the rabbits and harvesting the honey from the nests. Sometimes, the teacher would harvest the honey and would distribute the beehive among his students.

I left my beloved Putla after I completed secondary school in June of 1977. Like many young people in Putla, my three younger siblings and I relocated to México City. As a student from Oaxaca, I became more political. That is, I developed a political awareness by becoming an anti-establishment and anti-imperialist student. In fact, my political life and *comunalidad* blossomed in México City where I was planning to study medicine.

A few months after I arrived in the city, I enrolled in the *prepa popular* (a popular preparatory school that emerged during the student uprising in 1968), affiliated to the National Autonomous University of México (UNAM in Spanish). *La prepa*, as we called it, was an alternative school located in an old building with three floors that the students took over in 1968. When I was in my first year of preparatory school, I met Angelina and Hugo, who quickly became my best friends. Because *la prepa* did not receive funds from the state, we did not have paid teachers. The teachers were older students who would volunteer from the UNAM to teach us. There I met teacher Héctor, who was in his third year studying political economy in UNAM.

To sustain the university, we were all obliged to do fundraising. So, Angelina, Hugo, and I would ride the public buses and ask for donations. Many times, they asked me to deliver the speech. I would start my speech with "*Buenas tardes señoras y señores, somos estudiantes de la prepa popular número seis, y venimos a pedir su ayuda. Nuestra escuela existe con las donaciones que ustedes tan generosamente nos dan"* (Good afternoon, we are students from the popular preparatory school number six, and we come to ask for your help. Our school exists with your generous donation). While I said the little speech, my friends would take an empty Coca-Cola can to collect donations. People would give us a peso, 50 cents, or any spare change. Sometimes, we would collect $10 or $20 in pesos in a few hours. This money would be brought to the president of the school to buy supplies for the *prepa popular*.

One day, Héctor, my favorite revolutionary teacher, invited me to go on a march in front of the United States Embassy in México City. Hundreds of people came to the demonstration organized by the Mexican Communist Party (PC) to demonstrate against the United States' embargo on Cuba. As a sympathizer of the Cuban Revolution and member of the PC, Héctor had attended many political demonstrations. When Héctor asked me to go with him, I accepted the invitation without hesitation. On the day of the march, we met in the subway and walked to the march. He advised me to not let go of his hand and to follow his recommendations. I was not afraid to go to the march because Héctor was a veteran demonstrator. Although I was new to this kind of political meeting, I trusted him. After a long walk, we met with the demonstrators who gave us some "Yankee Go Home" banners. Héctor kept hold of my hand while we marched on the streets of México City screaming, *"El pueblo unido jamás será vencido"* (The people united, shall never be defeated).

As we were walking with hundreds of demonstrators, we suddenly saw the police mounted on big horses. Héctor nodded to me, pointing at the horses with his head while he squeezed my hand. He whispered, "Do not let my hand go. When I tell you, run with me." Despite Héctor's peaceful and calm whisper, I was afraid. The 1968 student massacre in Tlatelolco came to my mind, and my hands became cold. I was afraid to see so many horses stomping and neighing at the same time. The damned horses were so close to me! In México City, and in the *prepa popular*, I found my political identity living in exteriority, or outside of the system, criticizing the power of the state and imperialist policies.

Conclusion

As a child and adolescent living in Putla, I learned the power of *comunalidad* in shaping my cultural and political identity in relation to the town, the neighborhood, and family. In my memories, my migrant mother, or in her absence my *nanas doña* Estrella and *doña* Sole, sent me to the *tianguis* to buy food as they cared for my siblings and me. The *tianguis* and the marketplace enveloped me in a community of comfort foodways, social relations, and emotional experiences of caring, nurturing, sharing, and belonging in Putla, the town, and the semi-tropical space. This was important in the absence of my migrant parents.

Although Putla was relatively isolated, I was assailed to consume Western novels and Coca-Cola. At an early age, I learned that my town was part of the national anti-guerrilla policies of the federal and state government's secret dirty war against political dissidents. As a student, I became politically aware of the many injustices committed in my community, and the country.

In the global expansion of racial patriarchal capitalism, my grand-parents, parents, and some friends became an intricate part of the international migratory stream leaving Putla to México City, the United States, and Europe. Let me turn to this in the next chapter.

2
Fragmented borders and places

My four siblings and I sat in the United States Consulate office in Ciudad Juárez, México, waiting to say the Oath of Allegiance in order to receive our Green Card (work and residence) permit. Behind the counselor's desk was a big American flag and the photograph of President Jimmy Carter. The counselor told us to place our hands on our chests, near our hearts, and to repeat after him. As he began to say the oath, my younger siblings repeated it. I, who was almost 18 years old, stood there in silence, thinking that I was now a tabula rasa devoid of my sense of *comunalidad* and my history.

My mother told me about my grandparents, my father, and her life's history as an immigrant woman crossing the United States-Mexican border. When my family gathered to eat barbecue on Sundays, we reminisced about our experiences crossing the United States-Mexican and in-between border spaces. Intrepid men in my family led the way from Putla to México City, and from México to the United States where they became Green Card holders. Women in my family also crossed international borders for love as they relocated to the United States, Germany, and Spain. I identify as a Mexican immigrant woman rooted in three generations of family members crossing international borders where our *comunalidad* expanded to include millions of Mexican and Latiné immigrants confronting racial patriarchal capitalist regimes of violence in California and beyond.

Because my family and I immigrated with an official Green Card to the United States, our history crossing the United States-Mexican border differed from millions of Latiné undocumented people in many critical ways. While I acknowledge the privilege of crossing the border with a Green Card, the border was surely not a neutral space, but rather a highly emotional and traumatic space that created fractured modern neoliberal subjectivities and contested new cultural and political identities. Khosravi (2018) discussed the Iranian diaspora in Sweden as being fragmented based on class, gender, reasons for migration, and sexual orientation. In a similar manner, I employed the concept of having a fragmented identity because the border broke down and rebuilt my identity to meet neoliberal demands for cheap labor. I wrote as a racialized woman to discuss how my sense of *comunalidad* resisted racial patriarchal capitalist regimes of erasure and negation, violence, ideologies, practices, laws, and surveillance of brown bodies in its national spaces. I seek to understand how the border creates fractured identities and contested racialized immigrant identities and places.

"Grief and abandonment" is a section of this chapter that may trigger traumatic emotions. Feel free to skip it.

Migrant family background

My paternal family was fractured by the internal pressures generated by medical needs that could not be met in rural Putla,

Oaxaca. In 1961, my grandfather was working on the road connecting our town with México City when he had an accident. A big beam fell on his head, fracturing his skull. My mother and I, a newly born baby, flew with him to México City. My grandfather recovered from the accident, but he lost cognitive functions. Shortly, thereafter, my entire paternal family relocated to México City. My five aunts studied in technical schools (social work, nurse's aid, and bilingual secretary), but one became a professional seamstress. Some of my relatives were tailors, who taught my aunt to make wedding and *quinceañera* or sweet 15 birthday dresses in México City. I was a baby when my paternal family moved to México City, and while they would visit us in our hometown once in a while, I did not know much about their lives in the big city.

I was also a child when my parents relocated my two older siblings, Alfredo and Maribel, from Putla to México City because my older brother was sick. In the city, they lived with my paternal grandparents and my uncles and aunts. My older sister was taken to México City so she would be Alfredo's companion. As a teenager, my oldest brother would visit during his vacation periods from school and we would play marbles in Putla. I lived in Putla with my older brother, Andrés, who left for México City around 1975, as well as my two younger sisters and little brother. When Andrés turned 18 years old, he enrolled in the preparatory school and in the *servicio militar* (the obligatory military training) for a year. After I completed secondary school in 1976 in Putla, my siblings and I relocated to México City. All the siblings would go on to live together in México City until we began to immigrate to the United States. I had hoped to be able to study medicine in

México City and when the time came I was elated, but underneath I felt a deep sense of loss for my small town's *comunalidad*.

When we arrived in México City, we stayed in the small and overcrowded apartment that my paternal grandparents rented in Villa de Cortes, a middle-class neighborhood located close to the subway. I loved it because I could purchase my favorite snacks from the street vendors outside of the subway and walk home. The apartment was also close to a park, and I loved to play there with my cousins. A few months after we arrived at my grandparent's home, we rented a two-bedroom apartment near the international airport. From the roof of our apartment, I watched the Concord, literally, flying above my head.

While we lived in México City, my aunts rebuilt our sense of *comunalidad* by celebrating many national holidays. I recalled that my aunt would organize dinners to celebrate Mexican Independence from Spain on September 16. My siblings and I would ride an overcrowded Volkswagen vehicle to go to Ciudad Nezahualcóyotl to join in the national holiday. We would eat *pozole* and *tamales* or Oaxaqueño staple foods. I further remember that our apartment soon became a meeting place for young Putlecos studying in the city. My oldest brother's friends would come to our home every weekend, and my apartment would be full of Putlecos, varying in age between 6 and 20 years old. I was happy to see how our apartment became a space filled with young students, who joked, laughed, and ate together. My sisters and I cooked for everyone, and we would sit and eat in the small dining room. My new Putleco community, my new family, made me happy in México City. We lived in the big city for a few years after which we immigrated to Santa Marta, California.

The month before my siblings immigrated to the United States, I remember that my parents decided to take the entire family on a tourist trip to Oaxaca City, the capital of the state of Oaxaca. My father who had lived and studied in Oaxaca City wanted us to know the capital of the state where we were born. I recall fragments of our trip to Oaxaca. I remember that we visited the Nuestra Señora de la Asuncion Cathedral and I was very impressed with its baroque style. The interior walls of the cathedral were decorated with gold! My father then took us to El Cerro del Fortin, a large hill that overlooks the west side of the city, in his Ford pick-up truck. When we arrived at the top of the hill, the city was stunning. Oaxaca was such a beautiful city. I stood next to my father feeling so proud of being an 18-year-old Oaxaqueña woman.

After two days in Oaxaca City, we drove several hours to Puerto Escondido located on the Pacific Coast. My siblings and I slept in the back of the truck so we never saw the snake roads from the *meseta* to the west coast of Oaxaca. According to my younger sister Queta, we parked on the beach of Puerto, as locals called it, and slept there for three days. Queta remembers that we ate roasted *chapulines*, but she did not like them. While speaking to my youngest sister, I began to recall images of us sleeping on the beach and playing in the waves. My mother vividly remembers picking the *chapulines* in a nearby field and roasting them on the fire. She was sick that entire night. She did not know that the grasshoppers had to be cured before eating them. During this trip, I discovered my Oaxaqueña identity and that I liked eating tasty *chapulines*! I felt that my father's secret goal was to strengthen our cultural roots, knowing that we would have to deploy our sense of *comunalidad* many times in the future.

Fragmented Green Card holders

My family was further fractured when we became Green Card holders in the United States and in-between spaces. Anthropologist Seth Holmes (2013) studied an ethnic group, named Triquis, of undocumented migrants from a town near Putla. He referred to them as if they were new migrants in the United States. Oaxaqueño families, who are treated as if they exist outside of history, experienced erasures of pain and suffering. After the United States and Mexican governments signed the bilateral agreement, known as the Bracero Program (1942–1964), to import Mexican peasants to work in agriculture and railroad industries, many Oaxaqueños migrated to California.

My mother does not recall the exact year my paternal grandfather enrolled in the United States-Mexican Bracero Program, 1942–1964. She said that he enrolled when the war had just started. She told me my grandfather learned about the Bracero Program and traveled to the recruitment center in México, and later started working as a *bracero* in Salinas, California. She says that there were not many men enrolling in the Bracero Program from my hometown, but my father, my uncle, and four friends participated from 1955 to 1964. After my grandfather's accident, she recalls that only my father and three of his friends kept coming to work in California's farms until the end of the Bracero Program. After the Bracero Program ended, my father worked in my mother's stepbrother's restaurant in Stockton, California. My father obtained his Green Card because my mother's stepbrother sponsored him. By the late 1960s, my mother, my older brother Alfredo, and sister Maribel obtained their Green Cards too. Another family who were our neighbors in the *barrio de Arroyos* also immigrated to California.

My maternal grandmother, who separated from her husband, had one daughter and one adopted son. She then fell in love with a man who was in the State Police force, marrying him without much fanfare in Putla. A few years later, my grandmother, her son, and her husband relocated to the border town of Tijuana, México. They soon crossed the United States-Mexican border because my step-grandfather had a son living in Stockton, California. His son was married to a lovely Mexican-American woman who had sponsored his Green Card. A few years later, my grandmother, her son, and her husband returned to our hometown. Unfortunately, my mother does not know the reasons for my grandmother leaving and returning to our homeplace.

My father's younger sister Paula also emigrated to Germany in the late 1960s. She met a man named Hans, during the 1968 Olympic Games in México. She had gone to watch an Olympic soccer game at the stadium with her sister and friend from our hometown, when they noticed a group of young German guys. My aunt Ramona, who was working as a bilingual secretary in the UNAM (Universidad Nacional Autónoma de México), translated for the group. After the men returned to Germany, my aunt Paula became very good long-distance friends with Hans. They wrote to each other daily, and the friendship quickly turned into a long-distance emotional relationship. While Hans' letters were translated by his friend, my aunt's letters were read by my bilingual aunt Ramona. Despite the language barriers, a few months after Hans returned to Germany, he invited my aunt to come to his home in Frankfurt.

One day, she packed her belongings and left, leaving everyone and everything behind, for Germany. Although she was coming from one of the biggest cities in the world, she was surprised upon arriving in Frankfurt. Hans, who was waiting for her in the airport, took her to his home. Away from her *comunalidad* and without speaking German, or without any familiarity with German culture, my aunt felt lost.

Because my aunt was not able to communicate with Hans, she enrolled in night school. Within a few months, she could communicate with him. Shortly after her departure, my aunt married Hans in Frankfurt. The picture of her wedding proudly hung on the living room in my grandparents' home in México City. Paula's choices blazed a trail for the women in her life. After getting married, Rosa, her friend from our hometown, left México City for Berlin. The Olympic Stadium in México City was now very, very far away. Women in my family broke physical borders and cultural barriers for love. Relatively poor women from Putla, Oaxaca, challenged dominant narratives about Oaxaqueña immigration in the social sciences.

I too emigrated from California to Madrid, Spain, because I fell in love with a Spaniard. I met a man who came to study at UC *Tres Calmecac* with a fellowship from the Spanish Government. The fellowship had strings attached since it had a two-year home requirement. That is, he had to return to Spain after completing his master's degree. In December of 1994, we got married in Santa Marta without much fanfare and we left for Madrid, Spain, in March of 1995. We lived in Madrid for a few months, but he could not find a job. One of his friends told him about a teaching job at the Universidad Pública de Navarra in Pamplona, and so we relocated to Pamplona around September of 1995. The famous running of the bull's city in northern Spain was a relatively small and beautiful city. Initially, I was enchanted by the medieval walls and its Navarre cuisine, but I felt very isolated living in this city. I missed my siblings, *masa de chivo*, and corn tortillas. I did not want to live there for the rest of my life, and so I told my husband about it. We started to plan our return to California where my entire family had settled.

My husband and I decided to apply for his Green Card permit in order to return to California. In the 1990s, the United States-Mexican border had become heavily militarized and crossing without documents was extremely dangerous. Information from border crossers from Putla alerted me of the dangers of crossing without official documents. So, I did not argue much about it because I understood the danger of crossing the United States-Mexican border without legal documents. To fill out the Green Card requirements, I needed a sponsor with a stable job and good income so that my husband would not become a public burden. Then, I called my youngest sister Queta whose husband was working as a nurse to sponsor me. My sister spoke to her husband, a Filipino man who came as a child to the States, and he agreed to sponsor us. In a short period of time, she sent me a copy of their income taxes, so that I could include it in the application for my husband's Green Card. I mobilized my family to apply for my husband's Green Card in the United States.

One day, we drove from Pamplona to get a copy of the Green Card application at the United States embassy in Madrid. As I was reading the requirements to request a spouse's Green Card, I realized that I could not live outside of the United States for long periods of time. Well, my parents always said that I could not be out of the country for more than a year. Since I did not understand what they really meant, I kind of ignored their advice, but they were absolutely right. I could not be outside of the country for more than 365 consecutive days. If I did, I would lose my right to have a Green Card. In fact, I had to submit copies of all my Mexican passports to prove that I had not been out of the country for more than two years in the last ten years or so.

Before sending my Mexican passports, I counted the time periods that I was out of the United States month by month and hour by hour. I feared losing my Green Card because I did not want to live in Spain, away from my parents, especially, away from my siblings. I recalled that I asked my husband to help me count the time since I did not want to make a single mistake. One night, he took a pen and notebook and I gathered all my Mexican passports. For several hours, we sat together to carefully count the time that I spent living outside of the United States (visiting México and residing in Spain). When we had all the dates living outside the US accounted for, I was so relieved. Now, I knew that I had not been away more than the time permitted to live outside the United States. In my case, I was one month away from losing my Green Card. If I had exceeded the legal limits, I would have stayed trapped in Spain.

One day, I sent my husband's Green Card application package, including my Mexican passports, to the American embassy in Madrid. Three months later, my husband was summoned to the American Embassy in Madrid, and he got his Green Card. Unlike my parents, who waited a year and paid a lawyer, my husband and my one-year-old son obtained their Green Cards relatively easily. He had an excellent sponsor demonstrating that he would not become a public burden in the United States. I think that because he applied as a Spanish citizen, it made a huge difference in the Green Card application process. He was welcomed as a white, blue-eyed, European Green Card holder in the United States, and we came back to Santa Marta, California, in December of 1999.

My husband benefited from three generations of Mexican immigrants when he emigrated as a Green Card holder to the United States. He also benefited from my sibling's affection, compassion, and shared responsibility of helping family members. My paternal and maternal family became part of labor and love flows generated by capitalist economies and desires, but this produced emotional pain and suffering or fractures in my family.

The United States-Mexican border became a political war zone with thousands of Latiné people dying as they attempted to cross without documents. Jason de León's (2015) excellent book, *The Land of Open Graves: Living and Dying on the Migrant Trail*, documented the heartbreaking stories of migrants who died crossing the United States-Mexican border. My family and I crossed the border when it was not managed using military technologies and death as a deterrent.

Grief and abandonment

As a child of Putleco migrants, I remember that my maternal grandmother lived with us in the Blue House in the absence of my mother, who was working in California. I recall that my grandmother was a tall, slender, and beautiful woman who had curly hair. She loved to sit underneath the big bougainvillea on our patio to comb her hair. I would sit next to her resting my head on her lap, and I looked at the sky gazing at the clouds as they passed through the valley. Sometimes, my grandmother would bathe me or braid my hair. After she returned from Tijuana, she became very sick, dying within months. My mother thinks that she died of cancer. I have grieved her absence every day of my life. Oftentimes, I wonder how my life would have been if she had not died so young. Her husband, my step-grandfather, visited us in Putla once in a while. One day, he visited us with his cavalry chasing guerrilla fighter Lucio Cabañas. After my mother obtained her Green Card, she worked in California's farms from March to November for decades. When she returned from California, she would tell me to do the shopping in the marketplace and the *tianguis* and I felt special. As a migrant farm worker, my mother had social agency.

My mother made great efforts to minimize emotional fractures by creating a communal group of women who nurtured us in her absence. My mother would always employ a *nana* while she worked picking fruits and vegetables in California. Among many women who took care of us, I remember especially my *nana*, *doña* Estrella, who was a wise Indigenous woman. *Doña* Estrella would cook, clean the house, and wash our clothes. She did many other social reproductive tasks, domestic chores, while she cared for us. I remember her because of her amazing healing powers as a *curandera*. Every time that I fell ill, she would perform *una limpia* (cleansing rite) in front of her altar. She would rub my body with medical herbs and one egg, pray, and spray *aguardiente* on me. In this manner, she would bring my soul back again, and again, whether I fell or did not eat her food. Living with her, I felt safe because she never screamed or punished me. One day, she suddenly disappeared from my life and I was too young to ask about her.

I also remember my other *nana*, *doña* Sole, who came from a small village near Putla. *Doña* Sole was a short woman who would sew her own dresses. She would sit underneath the red bougainvillea on the patio of my Blue House and I would sit next to her. I loved to watch her stitching the sleeves of her dress. Every Sunday morning, I recall that her older daughter and her son-in-law visited her. They would sit on the porch or the living room of the Blue House to talk. Many times, they would bring her sweet sugarcane and ripe mangoes. They would say bye after a while and would return the next week. When they did not come to visit her, *doña* Sole's younger daughter would visit her. When I saw mother and daughter talking and laughing together, I missed my dearest and beautiful mom. I also felt envious because my mother was not at home. I felt abandoned in the absence of my mother! Despite my mother's efforts, capitalism robbed me of my right to be nurtured by my mother.

My mother, who left her seven children in Oaxaca/México City, recalls leaving México as a very, very painful, emotional experience. She remembers that when she first came to California, she was unemployed for one month. She cried every single day! One day, my father Pedro told her, "*te tienes que conformar porque te vas a enfermar*" (you must find comfort or you will get sick). She says, "He was right, I got sick." He took her to the doctor, and he spent a week's worth of wages. She repeats with tears in her eyes, it was so hard! Every time that I left Oaxaca, she tells me, I could not stop crying for long periods of time. She carried a heavy burden since she left a total of seven children in Putla and México City. She embodied regimes of violence and she became the perfect neoliberal childless mother-worker (see next chapter).

My poor mother remembers that crossing the international border was always a very difficult economic and social experience. On one occasion, she tells me,

> when I was traveling by myself, I had such a terrible time. One day, I sent a telegram to Pedro [my father] telling him that I was arriving on such-and-such date to Stockton, California. Then, I departed from Putla, Oaxaca, and went to México City to briefly visit my sister-in-law. It must have been early March, so that I could start working upon arriving in Stockton.

In México City, she purchased the plane ticket and flew to Los Angeles, California. She tells me:

> I was bringing just enough money to purchase the bus ticket from Los Angeles to Stockton. Upon arriving at the international airport, I was so hungry that I decided to purchase *una manzana roja* [a red apple]. *La chingadera* was that I no longer had enough money to purchase the bus fare. After I ate the apple, I asked myself, now what?

She did not have enough money to continue her journey from Los Angeles to Stockton.

My mother Guilla was wearing a very pretty gold chain which she tried to sell to fellow travelers in the bus station. Nobody wanted to buy it. Every single time that she offered the chain to a fellow traveler, she felt embarrassed. She says, "Nobody wanted it to buy my gold chain! I felt a stabbing in my heart!" Then, she began crying when an old Mexican lady approached her. "Why are you crying?" she asked her. Guilla explains, "I told her my sad story." The woman left and returned with her daughter-in-law a few minutes later. She told them her story again and they left. A few minutes later, the two women came back with an older man, "la *viejita* [old lady's] husband, I suppose". The man told her, *"le aseguro que su esposo no recibió el telegrama"* (I assured you that your husband did not receive the wire). He said, taking pity on me, "give me your money". "He came back with my bus ticket to Stockton!" Guilla found a compassionate family who took pity on her sorrowful and poor state. To reach the end of her journey, my mother built a sense of *comunalidad* creatively as she encountered many good people on the road.

This was a Mexican family traveling for work to Sacramento, California. When it was time to board the bus, they told her, "Let's go, *doña*." During the trip from Los Angeles to Stockton, the family took their lunch out and they offered her tacos. Guilla felt so embarrassed to the extent that she did not take any. Although she was so hungry, she did not eat their food. Hours later, when they arrived in Stockton, the old man offered her five dollars. Guilla took the money because she had almost nothing. With the money, Guilla says, "I purchased *una barra de pan bimbo y mayonesa* (bread and mayonnaise) to eat, and I purchased clothes to work." Like my mother, I too would cry and grieve her absence every day. (The following section was a traumatic event, please proceed with caution.)

I remember that as a child I would sit on the mango's swing of my Blue House every afternoon. Don Felipe, who rented my paternal grandfather's house, would sometimes push me in the swing. When he did, my skinny body flew into the air. My long uncombed hair moved with the force of the wind. I felt like a dove flying free! I would laugh so loud. I loved the swing that my father built for us in the tallest mango tree planted in the back-yard of the Blue House. The mango tree witnessed my sorrow, my pain, my childhood without my hard-working mother.

Sometimes, I would sit on the swing and scream my mom's name: ¡Guilla! Guilla! A tear would roll down my cheeks to no avail. Don Felipe would hear me and he would come out of his house to tell me to scream louder. I obeyed him: ¡Guilla! ¡Guillaa! ¡Guillaaa! The scream did not even have an echo, and I would cry silently. Sometimes, I would curse the bus who took my mom away. *¡Maldito autobús que se llevó a mi mamá!* (damned bus that took my mom). My eyes filled with tears and my small body trembled. As I flew into the air, I would hold tied with my sweaty hands on the swing's rope. I would hold on to the rope with one hand and clean my tears with my little skirt using the other hand. I did not know if my mother was alive or dead. I did not know why she was not there to hear my poems on Mother's Day. I was too young to understand the sense of grief and abandonment that accompanied me in the absence of my mother. I lived in the zone of nonbeing as a negated child of immigrants.

Because my mother and father were not at home in Putla, I felt abandoned by them. As a child, I did not know the reason for their absence. I did not know that Oaxaca was very poor, nor did I know that they were migrant farm workers in the United States. My parents would mysteriously disappear from one day to the next. In fact, I don't have a single recollection of saying bye to them. I knew that they would return based on the reddish colors of the sky in fall. That is, I did not know that they left from March to October to work in California every year. I could only tell that they were not at home. *¡El norte se llevó a mi mama!* (the North took my mom from me). It swallowed her, leaving an open wound down deep in my heart. My embodied pain and suffering experience did not exist as racial capitalism turned a housewife into a perfect, childless, seasonal migrant farm worker.

Fear and silence

Oftentimes, my family speaks about the politics of the international border when we gather to eat in my parents' home in Santa Marta. My older brother Andrés always tells us about his experience crossing the United States-Mexican border. After he completed his obligatory military training in México City, he decided to reunite with my parents in California. He was about 18 years old, sharing the collective responsibility of supporting two households: one in México and one in California. The United States-Mexican border is present in our quotidian and intimate life.

Andrés remembers that he crossed the United States-Mexican border with a *coyote* because he did not have a Green Card. In 1977, my brother arrived in Tijuana and briefly stayed in a motel. One night, he crossed the mountains by walking at a fast pace with the *coyote* who knew the tricks for crossing without being seen by the US Border Patrol. In the middle of the night, Andrés crossed the border and ran for hours, making it safely to the other side of the US-Mexican border. My parents, who were waiting for him in San Diego, quickly picked him up. After they reunited with him, they took him to Santa Marta, California. Like other members of my family, my brother became an undocumented deportable person, yet he was never deported to México even though the border patrol would frequently raid the farms. Similar to millions of undocumented persons, he could not go to México without a Green Card. He, and my parents, were trapped in California's zone of nonbeing without political rights or mobility. Then, my parents hired an immigration lawyer to help them file an application to obtain his Green Card. The lawyer recommended to my parents to apply for the Green Card of their children who were living in México City. My parents wrote to my older brother, giving him specific and detailed instructions of all the documents and medical exams we needed to apply for our Green Cards. Although my friends and I demonstrated in front of the US embassy in México City, I found the embassy to be an unpleasant place to turn in our application for the Green Card.

In November 1979, we traveled to the northern border arriving at the bus station in the United States-Mexican border town of Ciudad Juárez. We traveled 1,127 miles from México City to Ciudad Juárez. It took approximately 20 hours or longer because the bus would stop to load and unload passengers in many cities along the route between México City and Ciudad Juárez. As we stepped off the bus, my stiff legs could hardly move. As soon as I saw my parents waiting for us at the bus station in Ciudad Juárez, I forgot all about my legs. My parents and my brother had finished the working season in California, and met with us at the US-Mexican border. Because we were very tired from the long journey, we stayed in a hotel near the American Consulate office in Ciudad Juárez. Actually, I remember that we walked from the hotel to the Consulate office.

The American consul gave my father several sealed yellow envelopes after he interviewed all of us in his office. He told him to give the envelopes to the Immigration Officer at the US border. We left the Consulate office and walked back to my father's Ford truck. Immediately, he drove to El Paso where we waited behind other cars. A little later, after my father's performance of silence, obedience, and non-threatening posture, he gave the envelope to the border agent checking Green Cards. The agent opened the envelope one-by-one with all the tranquility in this world. The agent asked my parents and my older brothers to see their Green Cards. He carefully and tediously inspected their Green Cards, then, he turned to the children in the back of the track. The agent called out our names one by one. Without looking at me, he called my name while he held my Green Card in his right hand. I was afraid, but I managed to reply with a fearful monosyllabic, "yes". My entire body felt a deep painful void as if my soul left it!

When the Immigrant Officer finished inspecting the new five Green Carders, he said, "go", returning all the Green Cards to my father. The five new Green Carders, parents, and older brother and sister entered as legal residents in the United States. Now, the family could legally cross the US-Mexican border with permission to live and work anywhere in the country. My father happily sped away from *la garita* after we passed the border inspection ordeal. Unlike millions of Mexican and Latiné people, I did not swim my way across rivers or take dangerous treks in the desert. Although the US-Mexican border was relatively friendly, I was terrified. The unknown was too much to bear when you are 18 years old. I can't imagine how my little brother who was six years old felt.

My father, our hero and guide, drove to a fast food restaurant in El Paso, Texas. He parked his truck, heavy with its human traffic, at a McDonald's restaurant. My dear father, who could barely speak English, ordered eight hamburgers, French fries, and Coca-Colas. One big, really big, order for each one of us. When we got our hamburgers, I felt nausea. Sweet and salty flavors invaded my mouth, entering my small Oaxaqueña body. When the McDonald's red tomato sauce dripped through my fingers and my mouth, I did not like McDonald's hamburgers or Coca-Cola. I remember walking into the restaurant and I was stunned by the shining floors. They were so immaculately clean, and people were standing in line to order their food. People were standing in line! With every bite at my hamburger, cowboy country was so distant and vastly different from the snake-like terrace roads leading to my sweet home place. I watched the white customers wearing hats and cowboy boots waiting in line. These cowboys reminded me of the books of Estefanía which I had avidly read in my home place not long ago. Among many novels circulating widely in my hometown, Estefanía was a great western novel where cowboys conquered the American West. I was now standing in front of live cowboys.

I was eager to leave El Paso because it was very cold in November. Temperatures were already very low and my father's truck had frozen windshields. Coming from semi-tropical Putla, and México City, I had never seen ice collect on a truck. I recalled that México City was colder than my hometown, but El Paso was even colder. I hated it! Surprisingly, my parents had blankets and pillows on the back of the truck, yet we were shivering driving south to México City. As we were returning to one of the world's biggest cities, the flat, desertic, and almost lifeless roads of the northern part of México contrasted sharply with the rough terrain of tall, snake-like mountain roads of La Sierra Madre in Oaxaca. As we slept our way back to México City, we did not speak, not even once, about us having Green Cards. I do not think that we knew the meaning of having crossed the United States border to get our Green Cards. I supposed that we did not have much to talk about, so we remained silent. Three days later, we arrived in México City and my parents left for Oaxaca.

A month later, my parents came back to México City ready to return to California in January of 1980. They decided that we would relocate to California for the family to be united for the first time in many, many years. In taking this decision, they challenged the logic of racial patriarchal capitalist economies of having access to childless Mexican immigrant laborers. Now, we had our Green Cards and no obstacles to crossing the US-Mexican border. Around 3 a.m. on a Friday, we woke up and drank coffee and bread before we jumped into the back of my father's Ford pick-up truck. As we were seated in the back, my father came to talk to me. He said, "Guille, if you want to stay in México City so that you can continue your studies, you can stay. Think about it." Then, he added, "We will stop in the City of Querétaro or about two hours north from here. If you decide to stay, I will stop at the bus station to purchase a bus ticket for you to return to México City." My father made me feel special since he gave me the power to decide my destiny!

My father's serious tone of voice sounded like thunder in my head. I shivered and did not know how to respond to his generous offer to stay behind in México City. I just laid back and covered myself from head to toe with the blankets. My heart was torn into two pieces. I hated the idea of leaving México and I hated the idea of not being with my siblings. Two hours later, my father stopped at a gas station in the state of Querétaro. He came to the back of the truck and he said, "Guille, what are you going to do?" I said, "I am going to stay in México." He replied, *muy bien* (very good). He was happy to hear that I wanted to stay in México. He was hoping that I could study in México City. He told me, "I will stop at the bus station." He purchased my ticket and I left my sleepy siblings in the pick-up truck. I remember that I did not say goodbye. I just vanished. Like women in my family, I just disappeared! What did they think about it? Did they speak about it? Did they ask my father about me? My parents divided their family: four lived in California and three in México City. I joined my two oldest siblings: Alfredo and Maribel. In México City, I could study and build a better future than in California.

I arrived in México City around 9 a.m. and took a taxi to my aunt Nancy's home. A few days later, my older brother Alfredo came to visit my aunt Nancy. He opened the door and almost had a heart attack upon seeing me in the middle of the living room. He said surprisingly, *¡ay chingaos! ¡Ay fantasmas aquí!* (shit! there are ghosts here!). I vividly remember him asking me what I was doing in México City. As far as he knew, I had gone with my siblings to California. I took a big breath and swallowed a lot to get courage to tell my older brother that our father gave me the choice to stay. What will you do? he asked me again. I replied with tears in my eyes that I was planning to go to school. He said, *¡mmmh!* Unlike my younger siblings who did not have a choice, I chose to stay. He also had chosen to stay in order to finish his engineering degree at the National Polytechnic Institute in México City. Why could I not stay to study too? My older sister Maribel and her partner came to visit my aunt too and she was happy to see me.

I only lived with my father's older sister for six months because I did not like it. My aunt Nancy would get upset with me because I would go to political rallies. Every time that I went to a demonstration, she would tell me, "What if something happens to you? What would I tell your father?" I did not understand her anguish at the chance that I might be detained. My poor aunt was already living in México City when the student massacre took place in 1968. I arrogantly felt that she bothered me so much with the same stupid preoccupation. While I lived in Putla, no one bothered me with questions. My *nanas* had never asked me to explain anything, and so I had learned to be very independent. Now, I was not happy having to explain every single outing to my paternal aunt who felt responsible for my safety and wellbeing.

Slowly, I started to miss my younger siblings a lot. One day, I called my father from a public booth to tell him that I wanted to come to California. He was not very happy about it because he wanted me to study like my two older siblings. Nonetheless, he sent me the money to purchase a ticket to fly to Los Angeles, California, from México City. In August of 1980, eight months after my younger siblings, I arrived in Santa Marta, California. Scholars generally do not have access to discussions about family projects, reactions, negotiations, and decisions leading to leaving or staying in México because they gazed at poor Indigenous migrants from Oaxaca.

Marginal subjectivities

The United States Congress approved the Immigration Reform and Control Act (IRCA), and President Ronald Regan signed it into law in 1986, allowing undocumented people to regularize their residence in the United States. Under the law, any person who entered the United States without documentation before 1982 could apply for amnesty. It also required 18 months of residence in order to apply for the legal residence. Agribusinesses who employed a high percentage of undocumented farm workers lobbied for their inclusion under the new law. More than a million undocumented people obtained their Green Card in the United States.

As a documented person living in the United States, I remember the 2005 Sensenbrenner Bill (H.R. 4437) that sought to control the flow of undocumented immigrants by penalizing and criminalizing anyone helping an undocumented person. The Mexican and Latiné immigrant community in the United States felt that it was an assault on families, documented and undocumented, and communities in the United States. Since the 1980s, huge demographic shifts have occurred with the immigration of Mexican and Latiné people in the United States. Hence, Federal and State immigration laws, and local authorities, have sought to subdue the immigrant communities living, and working, in the United States.

Immigration laws sought to fragment immigrant communities. Living in the United States as a Green Card immigrant holder did not protect me from racial, patriarchal, capitalist regime of violence. Anti-immigrant laws sought not only to subdue the immigrant communities, especially Mexican and Latiné brown bodies, in the United States, they also served to create marginal and inferior subjectivities. As a Mexican immigrant living in the United States' zone of nonbeing, my family and I expanded our sense of *comunalidad* to confront the racial, patriarchal, capitalist, war against immigrants.

Surveillance

In Tres Rivers County, where Santa Marta is located, there were rallies and demonstrations against the Sensenbrenner Bill. Local Latiné leaders, the Catholic Church, Spanish radio, and *Television* (a Spanish-speaking television channel) encouraged everyone to participate in the demonstration. I did not need Jorge Ramos and Maria Elena Salinas from *Univision* (anchors of another Spanish-speaking television channel) or anyone telling me to be in solidarity with the immigrant community. I have participated in peace and anti-imperialist rallies all of my life. For me, this was a conscious political decision to be in solidarity with my community.

We carefully prepared to participate in political demonstrations in defense of our right to live and work without violence. I specially recalled that my husband wanted to make several signs saying "No to H.R. 4437!" However, we could not find wood holders, paper, or glue to make the signs in my home. We had to run to the store to purchase them. At the store, Mexican immigrants were buying material to make their signs, and many were purchasing Mexican and Californian flags. Although we had a difficult time finding material, we managed to make bilingual signs reading, "No to the criminalization of Mexicans!" The day before one of the big marches in Santa Marta, we found that my mother did not have walking shoes. So, we went to the store to purchase her a pair of tennis shoes at the last minute too.

On the day of the demonstration, my husband, my mother, my two boys, and I marched along the main streets of Santa Marta against the criminalization and persecution of the immigrant community. Usually, the marches were several miles long with hundreds of immigrants carrying bilingual signs and waving Mexican and American flags. We started to march on the streets of Santa Marta, and my husband carried my four-year-old on his shoulders. In our excitement, we forgot to bring the stroller, thinking that the demonstration would be a very short walk. He was sweating and resting for a few minutes because my four-year-old was heavy. While I held my older son's hand, who was about nine years old, we chanted, *¡el pueblo unido jamás será vencido!* (The people united shall never be defeated).

Hundreds of people came out to demonstrate against the potential criminalization of the immigrant community with the prison complex expanded to incarcerate undocumented migrants. In Santa Marta, the secret police dressed in civilian clothes were taking videos of the people marching in downtown Santa Marta. The tactic was clearly to make us feel vulnerable, without the right to demonstrate, and to remind us of our foreign status. We were subjects without legal or political rights.

After walking miles wearing new shoes, my mom's feet had blisters! When we arrived at Preisker Park, located on the northern section of town, she sat on the grass. Actually, we all sat on the grass because we were sweaty and thirsty. However, my mom was in terrible pain. During the march to the park, she did not complain because it was her moral and ethical obligation to support the community. She would say, "We are not criminals. Let them pick strawberries if they want." After we heard local Latiné speakers given their speeches against the Sensenbrenner Bill, we decided to walk back home. My mother could not walk with her bleeding feet, so we called my brother Andrés. He picked my mom up at the park and drove her home. For the first time in my life in the United States, I felt painfully vulnerable and powerless.

The state of California also had its anti-immigrant policies too. In 1994, California voters passed Proposition 187, also known as the Save Our State, which prohibited undocumented persons from using non-emergency health care, public education, and other essential services. In my view, the Save Our State proposition was an attack on the undocumented Latiné community. I could not understand Californian citizens who voted to approve the proposition. I could not understand how the most powerful country in the world could deny basic services to a community, regardless of their legal status. How could people be so narrow-minded? What happened to my federal and state taxes?

I felt so comfortable and safe as a third-generation Mexican immigrant Green Card holder living and working in the United States. Although I had many friends in the farm-working community who were undocumented, my family and I felt relatively safe from deportation. As a result of the national anti-immigrant legislations, my family and I deployed our sense of belonging and expanded our political rights by demonstrating against the status quo's unjust persecution of decent human beings eking a living in the farms.

Anti-immigrant legislations, as a means of legal exclusion, have been political scare tactics to create marginal subjectivities. Continuous attacks changed my sense of security and safety as local policies continued the racial attacks against the Mexican community in Santa Marta. Most importantly, I identified with the Latiné community. In other words, my sense of *comunalidad* expanded as a result of the anti-immigrant attacks!

"The Mexican problem"

Racial, patriarchal, capitalist violence also instilled fear, hate, and vulnerability that fractured my sense of belonging and place. In Santa Marta, California, anti-immigrant feelings were very strong too. One of the most vocal persons was George S. Smith, who sat on the City Council for 32 years, longer than Nicaraguan dictator Anastasio Somoza Debyle (1967–1979). Major George S. Smith, who claimed to be a "native-born" person, made frequent public comments saying that Santa Marta had a "Mexican problem". In his racist view, immigrants were destroying the city because they lived in overcrowded conditions in the low-income *barrios*. He declared that they would drink beer outdoors and that they were abusing the social programs.

Since Mayor Smith was reelected several times, he became a powerful rural *cacique* rooted in the local conservative community of an agrarian town employing thousands of Mexican immigrants, documented and undocumented, as farm workers. He could say anything against Mexicans living and working in Santa Marta without political consequences. He knew that the growing Mexican immigrant population did not vote. I felt pushed further down into the zone of nonbeing. Unfortunately, Major Smith's racist remarks did not fall on deaf ears.

Anti-immigrant and racist feelings were frequently published in the local newspaper called *Santa Marta Times*. Often, local people expressed strong hate against Mexican immigrants in the Letters to the Editor section of the newspaper. For example, a published letter to the Editor read:

> We do not owe these illegals a thing, and yes, they are taking jobs away from American citizens.
>
> Roberta Munoz.

Roberta repeated national tropes that "illegals" were taking jobs away from American citizens. Did Roberta Munoz feel more American after expressing her unflinching support on the "they are taking American jobs" rhetoric? I, who was working in the strawberry industry, never saw a single "American" worker. What was she talking about? I was not an illegal either. In fact, I was a third-generation immigrant with a Green Card. In the public eye, all Mexicans were illegals taking jobs from American citizens.

Other people publicly expressed the same racist feelings against Mexican immigrants in Santa Marta. Once, I was driving my old truck on the western side of Santa Marta where my house was located, and I stopped at the lights between Main and Blosser roads when I saw a white guy next to me. He rolled down his window and started to yell at me. At first, I could not hear him because I was playing the radio. Because the man was so agitated, he called my attention. He was screaming at me, "F***

Mexican, go back to Mexico." I remember thinking, "What? You go back to Europe!" I was so afraid that he would come out of his car to hit me. My entire body was trembling! I was so afraid of such a personal and racist attack. I sped away from the lights as soon as I could. Decades have gone by now and I still remember the racist incident. Did the white man feel better because he screamed at a young woman?

Every time that my family met at my parent's house, we debated the consequences of the criminalization and deportation threat. We did not think that we could easily return to México. My brother Andrés would ask: "What will I do in México?" He would add, "I will not be able to get a job, how will I support my family?" Like my other siblings, Andrés had three children born in the United States. However, deportation was an imminent threat because our friends working in the fields were being deported to México. Although deportations targeted undocumented people, we felt a great sense of insecurity and vulnerability. These deportations were intended to terrorize the Mexican, or the entire Latiné and brown bodies, community.

My identity as a Mexican immigrant was now a liability, my gender and the color of my skin had a different value than in Putla. In Santa Marta, I became an unwelcome and hateful Mexican immigrant woman living in exile, outside of the national and regional political territories that granted me citizenship rights and protections. I was further pushed into the zone of nonbeing, as a negated racialized human being.

I think that local and personal attacks became part of the low-intensity war waged against the working class, especially immigrant, Latiné people. I believe that the purpose was, has always been, to create marginal neoliberal subjects, to fracture collectives of immigrants, and to manage unruly immigrants and migrants.

Neoliberal citizenship

As a result of the anti-immigration tactics, the Mexican immigrant community contested anti-immigrant laws by applying for naturalized citizenship en masse. My parents, who were long-term Green Card residents, carefully prepared for the citizenship exam. Because they did not speak English, they feared not passing the American citizenship test. I cannot recall the exact number of months that my parents went to an elementary school, only two blocks away from my home, to learn English. They were very, very serious about it, going several times per week to study for the citizenship exam. One day, they submitted their application for citizenship to the United States Immigration Services. A few months later, they received a letter with the details for an appointment in Los Angeles. They knew that some of their friends were failing the citizenship test and they were very nervous. Nonetheless, they went to their interview as well prepared as they could be. Apparently, they had a sympathetic Immigration Officer who asked them easy questions. They passed the dreaded citizenship test! By 2002, all of my siblings and their spouses, about 13 people plus my parents, became naturalized American citizens.

However, I had mixed feelings because I did not want to become a citizen of the United States. I did not like thinking that I had to change the citizenship for fear of deportation rather than love for the country. My husband would tell me that it was best to have citizenship if we were setting roots in the United States. I thought that he was right, and so I filled in the citizenship application. I paid the fee and sent the application out. While I waited for my citizenship appointment, I studied the sample questions. A few months later, I received the appointment letter to appear in Los Angeles.

At the Immigration Office in Los Angeles, the officer who interviewed me was a Mexican American man. Some of the questions he asked were: who is the Governor of the State of California? Who is your Congressman? Do you speak English? I did not have problems passing the citizenship test, but I felt very sad. Was that political nostalgia? I had never voted in México, yet I felt sad losing my Mexican citizenship. Forced by the anti-immigrant legislation and racist attacks, I was dispossessed of my Mexican citizenship. I was grieving as if a loved one had passed away!

Tabula rasa

My immigrant petite brown body became a tabula rasa without historical memory. I remembered going to the citizenship ceremony in the Los Angeles Arena where I pledged allegiance to the American flag. My husband, my four-year-old son, my six-month-old baby son, and I drove to Los Angeles the night before the ceremony and we stayed in a hotel close to the arena. The next morning, we woke up really early and left around 8 a.m. towards the arena.

I recall that I entered a big basketball court where hundreds of Mexican and Asian immigrants arrived at the same time. Many were wearing their Sunday best clothing and waving small American flags. Like other immigrants, I sat in a chair waiting for the judge to perform the ceremony. I recalled seeing yellow cordons surrounding the area and security guards at the exits. I felt that I was glued to the chair. I could not go outside to see my husband and my kids. I could not leave to feed my baby son. Hours went by and I was slowly becoming restless. The judge finally came to perform the citizenship ceremony. He took five hours, or more, to come to the place where hundreds, literally hundreds, of new citizens were waiting for him. How could he take hours and hours to do a simple and very symbolic ceremony? If he was busy in court, why did he agree to perform a ceremony when he did not have the time? Waiting was part of the regime of violence and exclusion to make immigrants feel less worthy than white citizens.

Becoming a new citizen reminded me of my Green Card ceremony. My parents, siblings and I woke up very early to go to the American consulate office in Ciudad Juárez, where we stood in line waiting to meet the counsel. According to my younger sister Queta, we were first taken to a dark room. There, they asked us to bend over because they performed a physical exam. Although we brought X-rays of our lungs to the meeting, they still took another X-ray set and performed the physical exam. Obviously, they wanted to make sure that we did not have tuberculosis or some other contagious disease. They also wanted to make sure that we were physically fit. At 10 a.m., more or less, we entered the office of the counsel who asked us to sit on the chairs in his office. On the right side of his wooden desk was the photograph of President Jimmy Carter and the American flag, quite big for such a small office, I thought. As he was sitting behind his desk, he said that my two younger sisters, little brother, and I needed to take the oath. I did not know what the oath was about. I think that we needed to take the Pledge of Allegiance. As the American counsel was speaking to us, he stood behind his desk, closer to the flag, and we imitated him.

He put his right hand on the left side of his chest, next to his heart, and he said, "… I swear to defend the American Constitution … so help me God …" I think he said the Oath of Allegiance. Just like members of Congress do, I took the oath too. However, I am not really sure of what he said. Maybe he said: "I pledge allegiance to my Flag and to the Republic for which it stands: one Nation indivisible, with Liberty and Justice for all." I remember that as he spoke, my younger siblings repeated the oath after him.

I moved my lips in silence while I placed my right hand on the left side of my chest. How could I take an oath to a country that had stolen half of my *patria* in the United States-Mexican War (1846–1848)? I could not force myself to take an oath when the bald eagle had such a bloody history in Guatemala with the orchestrated overthrow of democratically elected Presidents Jacobo Árbenz (1951–1954), and Chile's President Salvador Allende (1970–1973). I could see on the wall, behind the counsel, the invisible face of bearded Argentinian Che Guevara. Like a tabula rasa, I had no history or collective memory, and I needed to pledge my allegiance to the American flag now. The counsel was either too busy with the little ceremony to notice me or he just simply ignored me. Clearly, I resisted inscribing my body with neoliberal patriotism that denied me full integration into the body politic.

I never thought that I was becoming an American citizen with equal and full rights before the law. In fact, the citizenship ceremony left very clear from the start that I was a second-class citizen. Did my new citizenship confer full incorporation into the body politic? Unlike Roberta Munoz, cited above, I did not feel like an American citizen. I did not think that I was incorporated into the body of the nation as a full and equal citizen. I felt so frustrated and extremely sad at the unnecessary and disrespectful wait. However, the wait was a *rite of passage* into a new citizenship which needed continuous surveillance and management. Nonetheless, I felt that the purpose was to create immigrant, inferior, brown, fragmented bodies that did not have much social value in society. In other words, the wait created second-class neoliberal citizens in the United States that were later inserted as wage and non-wage farm workers in California's thriving strawberry fields (see next chapter).

Wounded bodies

The United States has a culture that transforms documented naturalized citizens into wounded neoliberal bodies living in constant fear of deportation and surveillance. As a Green Card holder and naturalized citizen, I always felt fractured, existing in the zone of nonbeing, with multiple political vulnerabilities and insecurities. My older sister Maribel obtained her US Green Card as a teenager, but she resided in México. She studied social work and worked at the National Institute of Cardiology as a social worker. Then, she began her bachelor's degree studying anthropology at the university in México City. At the university, she met her husband from the northern state of Sonora and she married him in México City. She had two baby sons when she relocated to the state of Sonora, in northern México.

Because we did not know her boys, she organized a trip to Santa Marta, California, to introduce her sons to the family. She and her family drove just a few hours to the US-Mexican border. At the border inspection booth, the United States immigration officer asked my sister to empty her handbag on top of his desk, and she obeyed him. He then inspected all the items that were on top of the desk. He found a copy of a check stub among her belongings. He took the check stub and asked her to give him her Green Card. Then, he simply told her that she did not need it. He told her, "If you are living and working in México, you do not need your Green Card." So, he took away her Green Card! In this manner, my sister lost her right to live and work in the United States. Oddly enough, the immigration officer allowed her to continue her journey to Santa Marta. The power of the state left clear that immigration officers functioned as judges, jurors, and executioners. My sister's dispossession of her Green Card violated her right to be heard in court, the supreme law of a democratic society.

My sister decided to live in Santa Marta with my parents because her husband passed away a few weeks later. My parents advised my sister to hire a lawyer so she could ask for a special pardon to the Immigration and Naturalization Service in the United States. She hired the same lawyer who helped me and my siblings with the Green Card application. A few years later, she and her two young sons got their Green Card again. My sister's incident with losing her Green Card taught my family a lesson on insecurity. We were always at the arbitrary whim of the Border Patrol agents. We lived with fear, knowing that we could lose our Green Card without a legal hearing in violation of immigrant legal rights. The

Green Card placed Mexican immigrants under the constant panoptic surveillance of the state.

One year, my siblings and I went to San Diego. We wanted to visit the famous San Diego Zoo. As we were standing on the train station along with many other white and brown tourist people, a white woman wearing a black suit approached me. I saw her coming directly at me. She then stood a few centimeters from where I was standing with my siblings. She literally whispered to me, "Where is your Green Card?" I was taken aback. First, she was speaking to me so close to my face that I was afraid of her proximity. Second, she placed her hands on her hips while she was whispering at me. This was a clear gesture of white power! I was scared since I had never seen a white woman so close to me, nor have I ever seen a female immigration officer in my many years living in the United States. I only managed to utter, "why?" She then took a step closer to me saying "If you do not show me your Green Card, I will arrest you." I was threatened with an arrest because I dared ask the reason for wanting my Green Card. Even though I felt angry, I remained silent. I behaved as a well-mannered young Mexican immigrant woman.

My older sister who was standing next to me said, *enseñale tu tarjeta verde* (show her your Green Card). I searched in my wallet and showed her my American Green Card. She took it and carefully examined it. She then asked me for my personal information. I told her my name and that I was born in Oaxaca, México. I am a legal Green Card holder. She gave it back to me and stared at me with hate. I stared back knowing that she could not arrest me thinking, *hija de la gran chingada* (son of a bitch). No one at the bus stop noticed that I had just been selected for an immigration inspection. A white elegant woman in a black suit looked down at me: an Green Card holder ready to board the train. Although I was a legal Green Card holder, I felt as thought I was inhabiting a fractured and racialized immigrant body that did not belong neither here nor there. As a racialized immigrant woman near the border, I dwelled in a legal yet simultaneously an illegal Latiné body.

One year, after we became Green Card holders, my siblings and I went to the border town of Tijuana, México, for a few days. Although Tijuana was not Putla or Puerto Escondido, not even remotely, it was still México. My poor parents could not afford to take the entire family to Oaxaca, so we were feeling nostalgia for Mexican food, music, and arts and crafts. So, my sisters and I saved money and went to Tijuana.

My older sister, my two younger sisters, and my youngest brother took the train to San Diego which took eight hours from Santa Marta. We stayed in a hotel in San Diego, and we woke up early to go to Tijuana. We took turns to take a shower and dressed in our Levi jeans. I put on my new Nike shoes. I remember that we were very happy walking in downtown Tijuana looking at the handicrafts sold by street vendors. Then we ate tasty *pozole* and homemade *tamales* in a Mexican restaurant. The *mole* reminded me of elegant weddings in Oaxaca, but here we were eating tasty *mole* as an everyday food.

We walked right in front of a group of men who were sitting on the corner of a busy street in downtown Tijuana. When they saw my sisters and I, they started to imitate a cat's cry saying, "miaow, miaow, miaow". We ignored them, of course, but then I asked my older sister, why did they miaow to us? My sister said, Don't you know? No, I replied, perplexed at the cat cry. Well, my sister replied, they are imitating cats because most Mexican women crossed the border to work as *gatas*. I turned my head back to see them, and I said, "jerks". I never forgot this incident because I was very affected by at the male gaze and the sexualized and working-class joke that turned us into cats.

In the 1960s, the Mexican Miracle attracted Indigenous women from Oaxaca who migrated to México City to work in the informal economy. The expansion of the Mexican middle class opened up job opportunities inside the households of women who needed domestic employees. So, the gender and racist stereotype of Oaxaqueñas was insulting and denigrating, but it illustrated their conceptions of Mexican immigrants living in the United States. My sisters and I inhabited two simultaneous borders as insiders and outsiders, or Us vs. Them, white vs. brown, poor vs. rich in the United States and in México. The border was a place of cultural meaning reinforcing racial, class, gender hierarchies to remind people of their place in patriarchal capitalist societies that create social order along racial lines.

Porous borders

Although I have been living in the United States for about four decades, I still maintain my emotional connections with my family and *comunalidad* in México. It is through this emotional connection that I heard about my cousin's husband's kidnapping story. My mother and I have also discussed this event over coffee and bread many times.

My cousin Laura's husband Ramón had a frightening *secuestro* express while they lived in México City. Laura and her husband are both chemists who worked for a German transnational pharmaceutical company for several years. One day, the company fired her husband for unknown reasons. A few years later, the corporation fired her too. Laura received a certain amount of money as part of her severance packet. With her severance, Ramón set up a small factory producing soap which they delivered in and out of México City. The factory is a small, rented warehouse located about an hour north of México City where he drove every day. One night, he was closing the factory when three men came out to him. With guns in their hands, they forced him to get into a car that was parked close to the factory. Ramón was kidnapped for 24 hours more or less. Hence, the express kidnapping name.

Because Ramón did not have money on him, they drove him to several teller machines to withdraw his money from the bank. Because Ramón could only withdraw small amounts of money from each teller machine, they drove for hours around the city. When they could not take more money, they blindfolded him, taking him to an abandoned house outside of México City. Then, they called Laura demanding a ransom.

Because the kidnappers were bored, they played Russian roulette with him. They would put the gun on his head and they would pull the trigger. He would close his eyes, praying to God for mercy. The kidnappers played the roulette six or seven times. Each time that Ramón closed his eyes, he could only feel a tear rolling down his cheek. My cousin managed to gather the ramson and Ramón was released in an abandoned lot near the city. For several years, Ramón could not ride in a car because he would have panic attacks. I have seen him several times after the kidnapping, but I have never spoken to him about it. Years have gone by and nobody speaks openly about it.

One day, my brother Andrés received a phone call from his brother-in-law Juan who lives in the state of Oaxaca. He said that Juan called him, asking him, "Where are you?" He answered, "I am in Disney with my family." Juan asked him, "Are you sure?" My brother answered, "Yes", intrigued by the question. He told Juan that he was in Disney with his family. Then, Andrés decided to transfer the phone call to his wife Diana. Juan asked his younger sister Diana if everything was okay. Diana repeated, "Yes". Then, Juan explained to her that he had received a phone call saying that Andrés was kidnapped and that he needed to pay $10 million pesos for the kidnappers to free him. If he did not pay the money by noon, Andrés would be killed without mercy.

Juan ran to the bank, scared to death, thinking that my brother was in great danger. Because Juan only had one million pesos in the bank, he borrowed some money from his sister. Juan, who is a retired teacher, planned to sell five heads of cattle to raise the ransom amount. Because he was still short of money, he called his older daughter, a dentist living in Oaxaca City. Juan's daughter asked him to immediately call Andrés in California. After hours of sheer terror, Juan discovered that he was a victim of *del secuestro virtual expreso* (virtual expressed kidnapping) that was so popular in México.

In Santa Marta, my mother was also a victim of *el secuestro* express. One day, my sister Margot sent a text to the family chat room to tell us that my mom had been robbed of money. My nephew Tom answered, "Oh, no!" I was shocked by the information and called my mother immediately on the phone. "Hola *doña*

Guilla", I greeted her in my typical formal way. She replied, *hola hija* (hi daughter). "How are you?" I asked her in a solemn tone of voice, and she said to me, "Fine". I said in a very surprised tone of voice, "Fine?" I added, "My sister says that you were robbed!" She answered in a tired tone of voice, *si pues* (yes). I was very worried that she had been robbed, but I did not want to make her feel bad or embarrassed by the event. So, I softened my tone when I asked her, *pues, ¿que le paso, mami?* (what happened to you, mom?). Although we live in California, kidnapping stories have been part of the collective memory of my transnational extended family. Real kidnapping stories created vulnerable collective consciousness where people could die. So, after my sister sent the text to the group chat, my siblings and I arrived at my mother's home. We sat in a circle to hear her *testimomio* of her virtual expressed kidnapping story.

Around 6 p.m., two days before my sister sent the text to the group chat, my mother's phone rang. When she answered her phone a man said, "We have your daughter here. She has been kidnapped." My mom was very shocked to hear the man, and then, she heard a woman saying "Mom, I had an accident!" The man then immediately asked her to pay $10,000 dollars or they would not release my sister. Still in shock, my mom managed to say, "Let me talk to my daughter." You need to deposit the money now, the man told her. My mom explained to him that she did not have that much money. Then, he asked her how much money she had with her.

One moment, she said, and she looked for her purse. For a few minutes, the phone was dead silent. Then, the man demanded to know what she was doing. The man said again, "We have your daughter here! You need to deposit the money." My mom asked him to let her talk to her. He replied that they would not let her go unless she paid the money. She then told the man that she did not have a lot of money. He told her that she needed to find the money. Ask your daughters or your sons, insisting that she needed to pay the ransom. "Borrow the money!" he told her. After a few minutes, my mom found her small stash of money in her house and she told the man.

Afterwards, he gave her very specific instructions to wire the money to México. While he was on the phone with my mom, he told her to go to a Western Union store to deposit the $2,000 she had found at home. While my mother was driving to the Western Union store, the man was on the phone. He did not hang up the phone, not for a minute. After my mom deposited the money, the man told her to go back home. The phone call ended around 10 p.m. The next morning, he called her back around 8 a.m., insisting that she needed to pay the rest of the ransom. My mom, who was getting angry, told him, "Where do you want me to get the money? I cannot borrow the money because I will not be able to pay back." For my mother, who was an 87-year-old retired woman, saving money is quite difficult. Nevertheless, she had $2,000 to pay my sister's ransom. She did not think twice about sending the money to México. It was the safety and life of my sister that mattered to my mother.

To terrorize my mother even more, the man told her that he belonged to "El Cartel de Sinaloa and [he] sell[s] drugs". She asked him, "Don't you have a family?" He said that he had a wife and sons. Then, my mom asked him, "What kind of family man are you? You are involved in bad business and you will pay for it, and so will your family." He replied saying that he needed the money. "My sons", she told him, "are good men." She continued saying my husband and I educated them to be good men, *son hombres de bien* (they are good men). Raising her voice, she asked to speak to my sister, then in an act of valor, she *demanded* to speak to my sister. She insisted so much that the man transferred her to a woman on the phone. While she was speaking to the woman on the phone, my mother did not recognize the woman's voice. At that moment, 24 hours later, she realized that this was a sham! She then threatened to call the police, to which the man replied that the police were corrupt. "They eat from us", he said. "I might never receive justice on this earth, but you will be judged by God", she told him.

On Sunday, my younger sister Margot and her husband, my two older brothers, and I sat in my mother's living room to hear my sister's kidnapping story. We could not believe how easy it was to trick her into believing that my sister was kidnapped. I asked her, why did you not call my sister Margot? She told me that she could not call because her phone was busy. She was almost done telling the story when a policeman knocked on the door. My poor mother had to recount the story again to the police who took note. The policeman said that a lot of people were having the same experience in Santa Marta. He also said that there was not much that could be done. They could not trace the money. In theory, she voluntarily wired the money to México.

Several years later, my mom wanted to wire money and went to Western Union store in Santa Marta. At the store, the clerk told her that she could not wire money. I called the office and they said that the police had filed a report. Therefore, my mother was banned from wiring money to México. Now, she could not wire money to her best friend whose paralyzed husband could no longer work. Her friend was so poor and she depended on the wire transfers. My mother was banned from sending money to México, but so were her friends too. Adding pain to a traumatic virtual experience, this felt like a collective transborder punishment! Mexican immigrant families lived in fractured porous borders.

Conclusion

In my lived experience, the United States-Mexican border is not only physical barriers that separate two nation states, but rather this is a deeply emotional experience transcending national territories and spaces. As a third-generation immigrant with a Green Card, I crossed the United States-Mexican border in El Paso, Texas, with my siblings. However, I entered a social space as a Green Card holder where I felt vulnerable and continuously surveilled. As part of the Mexican problem, citizenship became not a desirable affiliation, but rather a zone of refugee against anti-immigrant policies seeking to subdue and fracture the immigrant Latiné community.

Naturalized citizenship became an important legal mechanism to enter the United States as a second-class citizen. The ceremonies, oaths, flags, and the wait created the illusion that one is safe within the States. In the United States, unlike México, I lived in the zone of nonbeing, without history and immigration rights. Racial, patriarchal capitalism needs fractured neoliberal subjects whose living labor produces wealth, as shown in the next chapter.

3
Living labor

I went to work in my parent's strawberry sharecropping plot the day after I arrived in Santa Marta, California. My parents and my siblings were picking mulch from the fields because the strawberry season had ended in August 1980. After lunch, I laid down in the middle of two strawberry furrows. I was so worn out that I did not mind sleeping on top of small pebbles. When my siblings saw me, they laughed at me! From one day to the next, I changed from being a radical student in México City to becoming an efficient neoliberal farm worker in California's rich farms.

Three generations of my Oaxaqueño family worked as *braceros* and family farmers, picking highly lucrative commodities in California's capitalist agriculture. To reconstruct my family's labor history, I talked to my mother over *cafecito y pan* (coffee and bread) in her dining room. I enjoyed the conversations with my mother who kept our living labor's history alive. On Sundays, when my family met for a barbecue at my parents' house, we spoke about our experiences in the fields. Although an abundant number of excellent books discussed the struggles of farm workers in the fields, this autoethnography blended family and personal histories to understand confrontations with racial patriarchal capitalism in the world's most industrialized farms.

California's capitalist agriculture depends on exploiting farm workers to withstand long grueling hours, rain or shine, in the fields. From my experience, farm workers' humanity is negated in a system that devalues immigrant bodies and life. Córdoba and Vélez-de la Calle (2016) argued that capitalist modernity had a universal project where it imposed capitalist social values and life. Building on Karl Marx's ethical critique of capital, Enrique Dussel (2016) explained the alienation of negated labor. Dussel claimed that capitalism is unethical because it exploits workers "without regard for the dignity of life" (Mills, 2018, p. 133). Dussel argued that living labor, as a victim, plays two roles in capitalist modernity: (1) as an exteriority, or alterity outside the system, to capital, and (2) as labor power functional to capital (id.). In this case, farm workers, as the "Other", are negated as human beings, yet they are exploited in their capacity (as labor power) to produce surplus value or wealth. I was heavily influenced by Dussel (2016) who stated that the suffering of the negated Other is the starting point of all ethical critique. From this perspective, I wrote a critique on how living labor (as *braceros*, farm workers, and family farmers) retained dignity transcending unlivable pain and suffering as a negated Other in an agricultural system organized to devalue all life. Like my mother before me, I find that my Putleca identity rooted in my sense of *comunalidad* endowed me with dignity, perseverance, courage, and respect, and it provided me with the strength to resist exploitation, asymmetrical power relations, and domination in the farms.

Oaxaqueño farm workers

I am a part of a multigenerational family from Oaxaca who has worked several decades in California's multimillion-dollar agricultural industry. Palerm and Urquiola (1993) explained that California's successful agricultural development has imported peasants, free of cost, from the Mexican countryside. My paternal grandfather learned to read and write by himself while listening to mules bray in the Oaxacan Sierra Madre. As an avid reader, he found an ad in a newspaper that the Mexican government was recruiting men in Empalme, Sonora, to work in the United States-Mexican Bracero Program, 1942–1964. He went off to work in the Salinas Valley's lettuce fields in California before recruiting his son Pedro, my father, and my uncle José, sharing information with a few of their friends to register in the Bracero Program too. Even though there were not many *braceros* from Oaxaca, my family joined the Bracero Program. After the Bracero Program ended in 1964, my mother joined my father in California. Our neighbors also immigrated to California, and hundreds of Oaxaqueños migrated in the mid-1980s settling in rural and urban enclaves in California, New Jersey, and other cities in the United States.

The Bracero Program and post-Bracero era relied heavily on laborers from the Mexican countryside. My mother Guilla remembers that my father Pedro was always contracted to work in Stockton, located in San Joaquin County, California, until the Bracero Program ended in 1964. For a short term, Pedro worked in a restaurant to get his Green Card, but he did not like to wash dishes. He always worked on the farms and he liked it. Pedro worked alongside Filipino farm workers who toiled in the asparagus harvest in Stockton. My mother remembers him saying he really loved working with Filipino men because they were "good workers", cutting asparagus on a piece rate (paid by the harvested unit). In California's agriculture compensation is structured to extract as much value as possible from workers by paying on a piece rate system. This gave the impression to my mother that Filipino workers were "good workers". For many years, my father harvested asparagus at a piece rate and earned good wages. When my father Pedro first worked in California as a *bracero* my mother was at home, in Oaxaca, caring for their older children in Putla.

My mother Guilla remembers that she came to Stockton, California, for the first time in 1964, in the post-Bracero era, and had to leave her children in the care of *doña* Estrella and *doña* Sole. I was then three years old. She worked in an asparagus packing house for a few months where she sorted and packed good quality asparagus. She was paid about one dollar per hour. After the asparagus harvest ended, she weeded out onions and potatoes in the fields. She vividly recalls that she also worked briefly in the packing shed sorting potatoes. Potatoes would be transported on a band, and workers would carefully sort them out. Unlike asparagus, she would get very *borracha* sorting potatoes. She explains that it was because the potato band was faster than the asparagus one. Once, the supervisor took her outside the potato packing house and gave her a new chore: cleaning wood crates. As a semi-mechanized harvest, potatoes would be brought from the fields with a lot of dirt, stones, and leaves, and she was assigned to remove all of the debris from the crates. In this manner, workers did not worry about the dirt on the band, nor did they have to manually remove dead leaves.

After the Bracero Program ended, women like my mother followed the working seasons in California. Because agriculture increased the production of labor-intensive crops, it was easy to find employment. Capitalist agriculture underwent a great social transformation as it became hierarchically organized employing foreign women workers without children. My mother worked alongside Mexican American women in an industry hoping to displace workers with machines. In the 1960s, farmers were thrilled at the technological harvesting machines displacing labor unions, unruly, racialized Mexican migrants, Mexican American, and Filipino farm workers who demanded higher wages and better working conditions in the farm.

Mobile labor

Capitalist agriculture depended on a mass of highly mobile fractured neoliberal farm workers without children. My parents, Guilla and Pedro, generally followed *las corridas* (also known as the circuit) of peach, pear, and apricot in the San Joaquin Valley. Between 1964 and 1975 my mother remembers that farm workers would work in citrus farms where they would be assigned four orange trees, and each tree had all the fruit ready to be picked. In Stockton the fruit would ripen at the same time because of the heat. The field boss would give her a light bucket which she would hang with a rope from her neck. She would pick the fruit from the branches, and she gestures as if she was picking the fruit from the tree, and she would put it in the bucket. When the bucket was completely full, she would climb down the ladder to empty the fruit in the big wooden crate. If the crate was not full at the end of her assigned trees, the forklift driver would move the box to the next set of fruit trees. Every farm worker had an assigned number that corresponded with a crate. That is how, she says, they kept count of her daily work. When I asked her which of the jobs (apricot, peach, or pear) was the most difficult, she said, "In those times, the most difficult thing was to move the wooden ladder because it was heavy and very big. I hated it because the ladder was very heavy." She tells me that my father "would help me". Like other farm workers, my poor mother had to endure strenuous physical conditions in the fields.

In 1967, Fresno County was considered the world capital of cantaloupe production. When she first arrived at the melon farm in Mendota, most workers were high school students. "I do not know the reason", she tells me. "Perhaps, there were no workers and employers brought students; perhaps it was the summer and kids were on vacation." After the Bracero Program ended, employers hired high school students and white women. However, they did not resolve the labor problem nor were they willing to work the long hours for low wages. Women like my mother would lean down to cut the melon from the vine, after which she handpicked the melons very carefully. She would then place them on the tractor that had a band on the back. The band would transport the melons to a crate that was parked on the side of the field. She became a "good worker" who worked 3,000 miles away from Putla, her children, and her family. In this manner, she had a negated existence as a human being.

In Stockton, my parents picked grapes for the wine industry and worked mostly with labor contractors. They worked in the same picking crew with Elias from Guanajuato and Celso from San Luis Potosi, México. When the grape harvest ended in Stockton, they would usually move to Calistoga, in northern California, to pick grapes for a few more weeks. My parents would be part of a working crew of eight people that was carefully organized to pick the fruit. A single row of grapes would be picked by two workers who cut big bunches of very sweet ripe grapes. My mother says with enthusiasm, "There were many grape farms there!" Although she picked grapes in Dolores Huerta's home-town of Stockton, she never saw the United Farm Workers union in the fields. Migrant farm workers who were subjected to the work discipline and super-exploitation in the fields never heard of the labor union.

My parent's living labor, dignity, and sense of *comunalidad* broke the alienation caused by daily exploitation in the fields. One day, she says, we were working on a farm and the labor contractor put us in an old dilapidated house. At the end of the working day, we went to the house, which was completely empty. Because I was tired from working all day long, I sat on the porch's floor outside. I noticed a few bees flying near me, so I looked up at the roof and saw a big beehive. I said to Pedro, "Pedro, look." I pointed at the beehive and I asked him in a sweet tone of voice, "Get me a little bit of honey." Although Pedro did not say much, he walked towards the vineyard looking for a tree branch. He then poked the beehive. Instantly, he saw the beehive flying towards him, and he ran away towards a nearby stream. He ran as fast as he could while screaming, "*¡Ay, ay!*" My mother was laughing when she told me, "I saw him running like a soul chased by the devil!" She added, I was laughing at him while he was running away. [It was so comedic that] I could not stop laughing at him! The bees stung him! On that day, our longtime friend Elias, from Guanajuato, and Celso, from San Luis Potosi, were staying with us in the same old house.

Elias, who saw Pedro running, was laughing at him too. Then, Elias proudly told Pedro, "You do not know how to do this!" Elias found rubber bands and put them on his sleeves. Then he put the pants legs underneath his socks. Right after, he found a plastic bag and perforated small holes to prevent suffocation. He placed the plastic bag over his head.

He took Pedro's tree branch and bravely walked to the beehive. He stood underneath the beehive and poked it. A cloud of bees zoomed towards him, and he ran away screaming, "¡Ay, ay! Help me, help me!" A few minutes later, Elias came back all stung in the face. The bees found the holes in the plastic bag! Celso, who was sitting next to Guilla, laughed so hard. Elias told him, "a little bit of respect, a little bit of respect". I was laughing to death, my mother Guilla repeated. While she told me the story, I saw tears appearing in my mother's eyes. My father and mother befriended Elias and Celso, and they remained friends for life. Sometimes, they even poked beehives together! In doing this, they rebuilt their sense of *comunalidad* to support each other in the contours of dehumanized farms that treated them like animals by housing them in isolated, rundown houses. They mobilized their social agency to engage the power of friendship contesting the objectification of their bodies. In their social exclusion, they actively maintained social and emotional bonds away from Putla.

Healthy bodies

Capitalist agriculture also depends on mobile, healthy, migrant farm-working people. In the late 1960s, my parents met Emiliano Alcantar and Ernesto Cervantes while they picked grapes in northern California. They became good friends with Emiliano and Ernesto who usually worked in Santa Marta Valley, California. They always invited them to come to the valley where employment opportunities were almost year-round. They would tell them that "work in Santa Marta was better. Wages were $1.50 per hour!" In the early 1970s, that was 50 cents per hour more than in most regions. This was a significant difference and Emiliano and Ernesto insisted that they relocate to Santa Marta. In California's highly advanced capitalist agriculture, friends built social networks, passing along information about job opportunities in other regions. After a difficult grape harvest, my parents finally decided to come to the Santa Marta Valley.

My parents did not have problems finding work because agriculture was thriving in the Santa Marta Valley. Farmers were intensifying the production of vegetables and fruits, needing more seasonal farm workers. During the spring and summer, my mother says, "Pedro and I would work weeding vegetables from 6:00 a.m. to 5:00 p.m." In many fields, the field bosses would give them a long hoe to clean weeds around the roots of the plants. Before hoeing the weeds, they would carefully sharpen the thin metal blade with a long filing stone. Then, workers would walk through every row planted with lettuce, broccoli or celery cutting out weeds with a precise stroke. She recounts that they also had to thin out extra plants like baby lettuces so that just one would grow to be big. This was a difficult task because the plants were very small.

Since my parents usually worked in small crews, they could not miss cutting the baby lettuce, or the weeds, with a single stroke. If they did, they would fall behind the synchronous crew. Workers would feel shame for not keeping up with the rest of the crew. Most importantly, falling behind could result in one losing a job. When a worker fell behind the working crew, the supervisor would help her/him to catch up with the rest of the crew, and the crew always had to move at the same rhythm or at the same level of exploitation. Guilla did not harvest vegetables like celery or lettuce because only men worked in cutting crews. My mother endured exploitation and gender discrimination on the fields.

The first fall living in Santa Marta, my parents found work in the *chile* harvest. Every day, Pedro and Guilla would arrive at the field where *doña* Antonia, the female inspector, employed them for the season in late November. *Doña* Antonia gave workers a five-gallon bucket and assigned them a single long row to be harvested during the day. My mother states that

> when you had a row with a lot of chilis, you would fall behind the entire crew. If that happened, you had to ask for help. If a worker had finished earlier than you, they would pick chilis from the opposite side of your row. Then, we would meet in the middle of the furrow. We would pick the chilis very carefully by leaning over the tree and cutting as many and as fast as possible.

When the bucket was full, the workers would empty it into a gondola or wooden crate pulled by a tractor. When the chili harvest ended a month later, my parents returned to Oaxaca, México, in late fall when the sky turned red in the evening. As a child, I sat on the swing of the mango tree in my Blue House, screaming their names.

My parents traveled back and forth between Santa Marta and Putla, Oaxaca, because they were migrant workers. This became such a normalized experience that I never questioned it. I never knew why my parents were not at home caring for us in Putla. In his autoethnography, Khosravi (2010) described his experience as an Iranian man living in exile in Sweden as something that stripped him of his culture, history, family, and home. I felt that I was stripped of my parents, their love, and their presence in my life. I felt fractured and they did too.

Doña Antonia, who worked for one of the richest men in the Santa Marta Valley, hired my parents to work at a piece rate (paid by the harvested unit). My mother says that picking chilis was extremely difficult. In Santa Marta, temperatures were very low and the chilis would freeze. She says, "My hands, my feet, and my nose freeze!" Although workers wore gloves to protect their hands, they would still get really cold hands. She states that her fingers would tingle and she could not grab the chili. The harvest was very slow during the early morning. Picking chili was also hard because workers had to bend up and down, up and down, so many times during the day. In many instances, workers would bend down to pick the chilis and poke their eyes with the tree's branches. She says, "That hurt like hell!" Besides the cold, chilis would dry out on the plant, and filling in a five-gallon bucket took a long time. *Doña* Antonia would inspect the quality of the chilis to prevent workers picking rotten chilis, dry leaves, or branches. In this manner, when farm workers picked unacceptable chilis or leaves, they were contesting super-exploitation, low wages, and capitalist work discipline in the absence of labor unions.

Between 1980 and 1988, my mother and I worked in a diverse women's crew on a farm owned by one of the richest landowners in the Santa Marta Valley. She says, "We toiled *escardando* lettuce and broccoli in a labor crew with four Mexican immigrants, one Texan, and one white woman. We were supervised by a white woman, called "Jinny", who always wore a *vaquero* palm hat, jeans, and boots because she worked with her husband in the horse farm owned by the same landowner". Jinny, whose husband was Mexican American, spoke a little bit of Spanish. Sometimes, Jinny would ask us, "How are you?", but she never engaged in long or complicated conversations. I remember that Jinny was a really fast worker in the farm, so she always gave us *carrilla* to work really fast. In the working crew, there was also a bilingual *Tejana* (Texan) named Estela who liked to work close to Jinny. Together, they made the crew run and I had a hard time keeping up with them.

There were also two sisters from the Central Mexican state of Michoacán. The oldest sister was undocumented while the youngest had a Green Card. They were very funny and I loved working with them because the day was short when they joked in the fields. The women would frequently say sexual jokes and would then sarcastically apologize to me. In the working crew, the Michoacana sisters helped each other a lot when Jinny made us run like crazy. I was the youngest woman and had less working experience than the rest of the crew. So, I always stayed behind the working crew especially when Jinny was present. I was conscious of the fact that working fast increased our exploitation and I hated it. Unlike the *bracero* era dominated by men, women were now working in gendered, segregated labor crews that were racially organized along age, citizenship, race, class, and language skills. My mother and I recreated our sense of *comunalidad*, or it expanded, through friendship in the fields.

Over countless coffee and bread conversations, I asked my mother Guilla to compare and contrast farm work between

Stockton and Santa Marta to elicit a critique of capitalist agriculture and she spoke about her living labor. In Stockton, she
tells me, "Upon waking up around 2 a.m., we would quickly
eat raw eggs and milk." Then, she would hurry to the central
location in downtown Stockton where buses would pick farm
workers. She says, "I would start working at 5 a.m. or earlier
and I would finish at 2 p.m." During the summer, because the
Central Valley was so hot, work days were shorter. In Stockton,
she remarks, *la vida era mas rapida* (life was faster) because they
usually worked on a piece rate system or one based on the
worker's ability to pick fruit as fast as possible. In other words,
the level of exploitation was extremely high. However, my parents harvested fruit trees like grapes and oranges and so they
stood upright most of the time. Their diet, level of exploitation,
and working conditions impacted their fractured, neoliberal,
and racialized bodies.

She added that my late father Pedro did not like living in Santa
Marta. Local farmers planted a lot of crops like peppers, strawberries, chilis among many other crops and they could work nine
months of the year. During this time, Pedro and Guilla found
employment easily. The winter season was very different. They
would wake up very early in the morning and would drive to
the labor contractor's hiring office. Upon arriving, sometimes at
dawn, it was dark and cold, yet they would wait in their cars until
the office opened. She explains, "Often, we worked a few hours
per day, eight hours per day, or a week." In other words, work
was sporadic! In Guilla's view, working conditions and exploitation (piece rate vs. hourly wages) made a huge difference in the
quality of their lives in Stockton and Santa Marta.

Between 1980 and 1985, my mother and I worked for a local labor contractor in Guadalupe, west of Santa Marta. He employed us to put rubber bands on top of the mature cauliflower heads. The supervisor gave us hundreds of rubber bands. Then, we took the cauliflower leaves with both hands and brought them together by tying a knot with the rubber band. We wrapped the leaves around the white cauliflower to prevent sunburn and pass quality inspections. My mother recalls that "a burnt cauliflower would have yellow spots on it!" We started work at dawn when the mist had not yet dissipated in the valley. To wrap the long leaves, we had to stretch all over the wet plant and we would end up wet. In the morning, even if it was cold, we had to work. At the end of the day, she says, "our arms bled a little because the rubber bands would scratch our skin". Frozen hands, bending, and bleeding arms were the capitalist markers of brutal exploitation and alienation of the farm workers living labor in racial, patriarchal, capitalist economies. Our living labor was the neoliberal victim in an unethical agricultural system that treated workers as animals.

Sometimes, we would find work on crops that were being irrigated with *agua rodada* (that is, vegetable rows were flooded and we had to work in wet furrows). My mom explains that "it was tiring to walk in wet, muddy, furrows!" Because the soil was wet, the hoe would collect mud, and it did not only weigh more, the blades would not cut the weeds. Walking was also very difficult because mud collected on the shoes. These would make walking very slippery and so one could risk falling and breaking a bone in the field. Wounded or fractured bodies would not be employed because their labor power was no longer productive in the fields.

Wounded body

Capitalist agriculture functioned without regard for safety in the workplace. One year, my mom had an accident while she was picking chilis in Santa Marta. In the chili farm, each worker filled the five-gallon bucket and walked to the edge of the farm. There, the bucket would be empty into a big container called the "gondola". Since farm workers were paid by the harvested piece, workers ran all the time. The faster they worked, the more they made in quantity and wages. As a result of the accident, my mother's wounded or fractured body lost its productive value as labor power, which was not useful to capitalist reproduction of wealth.

A few years after working in the chili harvest, my mom was sitting on the floor resting a little bit after several hours of toiling on the farm. She was seated in a position where she was not facing the tractor. She was very tired to the extent that she did not hear the tractor approaching her. All of a sudden, she felt the tractor ran over one of her legs! She screamed, "¡Ay, ay, ay!" My father Pedro, who was nearby, came running towards her. He grabbed her from underneath her arms and pulled her out. Her leg resting on sandy soil sunk, but it was trapped underneath the tractor. As Guilla was crying for help, other farm workers ran to help her. Guilla's leg did not break, nor was it swollen. However, she could not stand because her leg hurt a lot. Later, Pedro drove her to the doctor, but her leg was not even bruised! The medical doctor did not believe that the tractor had run over her leg. After the accident, she could not work and the medical establishment did not authorize her disability. Her body lost economic value, in terms of her labor power, but her living labor kept her going in the search for justice. Based on her sense of *comunalidad*, dignity, and self-respect, she sought accountability in the fields!

Although I was living in Putla, I remember that she would speak about *el careo* in court. My mother filed a lawsuit against her employer, demanding disability benefits and compensation for the time off from work, and for her pain and suffering. My mother stopped working for a few years because she had an open legal case against her employer. For a couple of years, she gave her *testimonio* about her accident on the farm. I would hear my mother saying that doctors would testify against her in court, hence the *careo*; and the judge would send her to talk to other doctors, but they did not believe her at all about the injured leg. Even though the leg did not break, she experienced pain and suffering as a result of the accident. As a farm worker, she sought restoration of her dignity in an unethical system that devalued her life and her injured immigrant female body.

My mother told me that one doctor sent her to hypnosis to learn the truth about her accident. I was surprised when she mentioned the word "hypnosis". I never heard that a farm worker victim would be sent to a hypnosis session to discover the truth. As a racialized poor woman, inferior foreigner, and non-English speaker, the medical establishment did not believe that she injured her leg in the farm. On top of her wounded body, she had to endure the dehumanization of the medical establishment! Regimes of power and truth were part of the violence imposed on suspected racialized bodies that jeopardized honest and hardworking farm workers.

Because Mexican immigrant labor is racialized in the farms, farm workers toil in unsafe working conditions. Guilla could not walk normally, nor could she work. As a poor migrant farm worker, she did not have an income or savings to support her children in Putla and México City. As a result, she decided to file a lawsuit against the employer, and went to court for three years. She said that the translator would drive her to the doctor and to court because Pedro could not afford to stop working. After years of going to different doctors and to court appointments, she won the legal case. With the money from the lawsuit, Guilla paid for her children's Green Cards and she purchased her home in Santa Marta. Guilla fiercely loved her children despite the long seasons of separation and she brought them to Santa Marta at the first opportunity. Guilla's living labor contested the objectification of her body and she regained her dignity and motherhood! She also rebuilt her sense of *comunalidad* as a negated mother who deeply missed her seven children.

Working families

California's agriculture also depended on poor working immigrant families whose labor exploitation produced wealth in an advanced capitalist agriculture. In Stockton, Guilla and Pedro saw entire families picking green tomatoes in the fields. In the late 1960s, women would bring their babies to the fields and would place them underneath temporary shelters made up of cardboard boxes. Many times, Mexican families would bring three or four kids to work in the tomato fields. The older children who were five or six years old would help their parents. The tomato boxes would be placed next to their assigned rows and filled with green tomatoes. Guilla remembers when workers would send their children to steal boxes from each other after filling up their boxes. Sometimes your boxes would just disappear from your row! She adds, "Children would work because the mothers would ask them to steal boxes!" Entire families would work for the meager wages and the work of children was imperative to the survival of poor, farm-working families.

Guilla and Pedro picked grapes with families from Putla who worked in the vineyards of northern California. Juan González came during the Bracero Program, like Pedro and a few more Putlecos, to work in Healdsburg, California. When the Bracero Program ended in 1964, Juan became a tractor driver in a big vineyard. A few years later, Juan's wife Petra immigrated with her children to Healdsburg. Guilla vividly remembers Petra and her young sons and daughters Maria, Lucero, Mario, Arturo, and Jorge harvested grapes during the summer. Another immigrant family, called by their nickname *Pelos* (hair), worked in the same vineyard. Guilla remembers that Mario would call out, "*¿Dónde están los pelos?*" (where are the hairs?). Someone would respond, "*¡En medio!*" (in the middle). Everyone in the working crews would laugh at the sexual joke.

In Santa Marta, working families became the backbone of the strawberry industry when Japanese Americans turned to sharecropping the crop to avoid labor unionism in the fields. Don Francisco, an ex-*bracero* from the Central Mexican state of Michoacán, became the field boss of a 20-acre farm owned by a Japanese American family. He carefully selected potential share-croppers who were not active with the United Farm Workers (UFW) union. He did not only choose fast or responsible pick-ers, he invited especially those with family members. Making an exception, Don Francisco invited Pedro to take half an acre of strawberries on shares because he considered him to be a good and extremely responsible worker. Like hundreds of families, they planted, cultivated, and harvested their strawberry plot from late October to late July, making this the longest, and most stable, working season. During the harvest, sharecroppers would receive half of the profits and an extra quarter for each harvested box of strawberries for the fresh market.

Sharecropping was a system of production based on equal shares where farmers provided the land and the inputs. At the end of every summer, all strawberry farmers tilled the land, purchased inputs, and fumigated the soil. When the farm was ready for planting, they would subdivide it into small plots. In September, more or less, each sharecropper would then be assigned to a small plot. By mid-October, my parents would carefully plant the strawberry seedlings on their assigned plot. By mid-November, they left to visit their children in Oaxaca, México. Miriam Wells (1996) wrote about the sharecropping system which she considered beneficial to families.

Families had to ensure that strawberries would pass strict quality inspections. When the strawberry harvest began, my parents picked strawberries mainly for the fresh market from early March to June. The fresh market required extreme hand-eye coordination and special selection based on quality standards of size, shape, and color. For instance, if they picked and packed a very small green strawberry, this would not pass the quality inspection for size and color. Therefore, every single berry was carefully picked and packed in a 12-pound carton try that contained 12 little green baskets. Each sharecropper did not only have the responsibility of picking strawberries, each was also responsible for inspecting the quality of the berries. If the strawberries did not pass quality inspections, the supervisor would reject the load. The sharecropper would not be compensated or would risk losing the plot of land.

Mexican immigrant families participated in a hierarchical quality system where Don Francisco supervised the quality of the berries two or three times per day. If the strawberries passed each quality inspection, the strawberry load was taken to the cooling plant. If it did not, the strawberry load would be sorted all over again, or it would be taken to the dump fields. After sales, Pedro would receive a 50 percent share and an extra quarter per harvested box. For several months of the year, Guilla and Pedro had steady employment and a certain degree of autonomy over the labor process. This was, however, hierarchized to ensure quality requirements, which global consumers demanded.

Brazos pequeños (small arms)

Mexican immigrant families relied on the availability of non-wage, young, and child labor to succeed as strawberry sharecroppers. In 1977, Guilla's third son, Andrés, who had just turned 18 years old, arrived in Santa Marta. Andrés quickly learned to pick, sort, and pack strawberries for the fresh and cannery market, easily surpassing his parents. However, Guilla's household had a problem now, as three people could harvest half an acre of strawberries in a few hours, workdays were now extremely short. The next season, they had increased their plot by half an acre. After the strawberry season ended in August, they went to northern California to pick grapes for the wine industry.

Guilla's sharecropping plot increased once more with the arrival of her other children from México City. In 1980, Andrés

(18 years old), Margo (13), Queta (10), and José (8) arrived in January. I (18) arrived several months later in August. During the winter, Guilla's three youngest children were taken to the fields to keep the strawberry plants clean of weeds and pest-free. The supervisors valued strawberry sharecroppers who kept their plots free of weeds to avoid pests and lower production costs. As non-wage laborers, Guilla's children played an important role in the sharecropping plot because they worked on weekends, off school days, and summer vacation, all without compensation. A few years later, Guilla's oldest son Alfredo, and daughter Maribel, arrived in Santa Marta, and they worked in the strawberry industry too. In two years, Guilla's household rapidly changed in size (11 members) and composition (gender and age differentiation). It had become an extremely reliable, flexible, non-wage workforce of neoliberal fractured Green Card holders. Child labor was the worst ethical violation employed in capitalist farms.

I went to work in the strawberry fields the day after my arrival from México City. My parents woke us up at 5 a.m. and as soon as we arrived at the fields, my father organized his working crew and I was assigned two furrows in which to uproot mulch. I stood on the edge of the field smelling the rotten aroma of decomposed strawberries, unsure of how to start. I watched my younger sister, Margot, lean down to take a piece of mulch and roll it into a circle before moving on. She proceeded to take another piece of mulch and I began to imitate her. When I pulled the mulch out, it smeared my face with mud. After a few hours of intense work, I sat in the middle of my two strawberry rows. I remember closing my eyes and feeling the sun warm my face. As a child living in Putla, Oaxaca, I stared at the dark clouds announcing a semi-tropical rain.

Now, I was sleeping in the middle of a capitalist farm. It really did not take long to fall asleep! After lunch, my siblings started to look for me and they could not find me. So, they called my name out: "Guille! Guille!" I woke up when I heard my name. My older brother Andrés asked me, "*¿Que, te cansaste?*" (what, did you get tired?) and started to laugh because I had fallen asleep in the middle of the furrows. All my siblings laughed at me. When I left México City to join my family in California, I never imagined my life as a farm worker. Like millions of undocumented and documented Latiné immigrant bodies, my racialized body had specific value by becoming a neoliberal farm worker at the service of unethical employers.

When the harvest for the fresh market began in the spring, my father Pedro carefully organized his family to maximize available non-wage labor in the plot. During the summer, older children and adults took one furrow to pick all the ripe berries whereas young children "helped" the adults. Guilla would stand in the middle of two furrows picking all the strawberries close to her, and her youngest son José picked the strawberries on the outer line, keeping up with his mother's work pace. He had short arms and could not reach strawberries well. Nonetheless, they would fill the 12-pound carton tray in 10 minutes. At the peak of the harvest, they harvested between 30 and 40 trays per day of strawberries for the fresh market. All of Guilla's children would pick strawberries that would later be inspected by Pedro and, ultimately, Don Francisco. If the fruit did not pass the quality inspection, they would be thrown into the trash. In this situation, the sharecropper did not receive payment for their work. As such, Pedro was very skillful at carefully deploying and supervising family non-wage laborers to keep up with strict labor demands during planting, cultivation, and harvest periods. He never had a bad quality load.

Because Guilla's family had more non-wage workers than needed on the plot, they soon increased the sharecropping plot to three acres. At the peak of the harvest in May, the family collected 200–300 12-pound trays of strawberries per day for the fresh market. My father Pedro was paid his 50 percent share after sales, usually a week later. Because Guilla's household had a bigger non-wage labor pool with the immigration of her children, they would divide it between non-wage and wage labor. My mother and I worked in the vegetable farms for a wage full time, and would go to the strawberry sharecropping plot later in the day. After working with the group of women, my mother and I drove to the sharecropping plot. We had two jobs. Women's labor power became functional to capital.

I did not like having two jobs and I always criticized my parents. I did not understand their poverty and their need to pull economic resources together in order to pay bills, food, and the mortgage of their home in Santa Marta. Capitalist agriculture benefited from social emotional bonds that kept families working together in the strawberry fields. That is, our sense of *comunalidad* built cooperation, solidarity, and affection to work in the fields, so I could not abandon my parents to their own luck. Even though I did not like working in the fields, I had to help my family. That is, my sense of moral and ethical responsibility and obligation to my family benefited agribusiness.

Caballitos (little horses)

I felt like a fractured workhorse devoid of my humanity, and my sense of *comunalidad*, as a young worker in the fields. My mother and I skillfully picked strawberries after working eight hours in the vegetable farms. When we arrived at the farm, we would take a *caballito* and mount two strawberry trays on top of each other. These would be filled with carefully picked red, shining, conical strawberries. Each strawberry would be placed in the same direction, this is called *la planchada*. Every single berry had the same color, size, and shape. Rotten or deformed strawberries would not be placed in the basket, but these needed to be cut from the plant. Behind each worker was a line of red berries thrown on the floor because they did not meet strict quality inspections. I never understood the waste! Plants were bearing higher amounts of fruit, but some did not pass strict quality inspections. Besides, I could work less if I did not have to pick bad berries. My sense of *comunalidad* steeped in nature—flora and fauna—could not understand the objectification of land or domestication of strawberry plants.

During the day, workers would bend for approximately ten minutes picking berries with both hands extremely carefully to avoid damage. When the first 12-pound box was filled, these would be placed on the floor. After picking the second 12-pound box, we would take them outside the field. We would pile them in stacks of ten. During the peak of the harvest in May, my mother Guilla would harvest a total of 40 boxes of 12-pound strawberries for a total of 480 pounds of fresh strawberries per day. Sometimes, she would harvest more or less, depending on production cycles and the plant variety.

The Oso Grande strawberry variety was a University of California patent released in 1989 that would produce close to 40 tons of strawberries per cycle. Guilla's family, who has been farming strawberries for decades, loved Oso Grande, but I did not. I hated picking Oso Grande strawberries. I felt that the harvest would never end no matter how tired my body felt. I felt that scientists developing new strawberry varieties lost the ethical train. The body of neoliberal immigrant farm workers was not taken into consideration when developing new plant varieties like Oso Grande that produced 40 tons of fruit per season. We were an inferior Other, our humanity negated, our fractured immigrant bodies exploited without regard for our dignity. We would have suffered less body pain; both the bodies of workers and nature were victims of an unethical racial patriarchal capitalist system.

Like her children, my mother Guilla would be exhausted picking strawberries at the end of the day. At times, my mother would accidentally place her injured knee on a stone and she would cry out, "¡Ay!" Sometimes, we would hear her, "¡Ay, ay, ay!" Her tearful voice would call the attention of everybody in the family. Whoever happened to be next to her would say, "¡cuidado mami!" (be careful mom). Guilla would stop picking berries for a minute while she would rub her knee with both hands. A minute later, she would restart the kneeling process, making her pain invisible. During the night, the knee that the tractor ran over would hurt a lot. Guilla's sister in-law would also kneel down to pick strawberries. However, she would bring a small thick rug, and would drag it forward before putting her knees on the floor. She would protect her knees from small pebbles.

My body was no longer a tabula rasa devoid of history, culture, and home. The strawberry industry required a neoliberal, racialized, exploitable, fractured, docile body to withstand the most unnatural and painful postures required to harvest a lucrative commodity. Farm workers would bend to the left and right to quickly pick as many strawberries from the two inner lines of the strawberry furrow. This movement and suspension would be done hundreds of times during the day. As time went by, farm workers had a more difficult time standing up because of back pain. Sometimes, I would start to stand up and would stop mid-way! I could not bring my body to a normal upright position because the back pain was unbearable. My body would hurt. Even going to the bathroom would hurt our bodies. The first few days of picking strawberries were literally a pain in the butt. As a racialized Mexican immigrant and young woman, produced at the US-Mexican border as a neoliberal worker, I withstood the daily pain, just like the rest of my exploited family. My Green Card inserted me into society as a productive farm worker.

As I fought the alienation of my living labor, I began to resent being a strawberry worker. When I first came to Santa Marta, I would take the best strawberries home. I would take a bunch and rinse them with cold water before cutting off the crown and splitting them in half. I would whip sour cream and sugar and pour the whipped cream on the strawberries. All my siblings would then eat strawberries as dessert. At first, they were so delicious, but as time went on I stopped enjoying them. The sweet aroma of the University of California's Camarosa, Oso Grande, and Chandler strawberry varieties gave me nausea. I hated smelling, touching, and eating Californian strawberries that sybarite consumers demanded all over the world. Strawberry commodities embodied my labor power, my pain, and suffering. My emotions, taste, rejection of strawberries symbolically contested the total exploitation of farm workers in the neoliberal capitalist farms.

I finally understood the reason my father did not want me to come to the United States. Like him, I would become an animal, a *caballito*, running all day long to barely eke a living out of miserable wages. My sense of *communalidad* did not only nurture me in an alien society, but it expanded to contest asymmetrical relations of power, exploitation, and objectification of the foreign body in agriculture. In the absence of labor unions to demand better working conditions, we symbolically challenged the logic, the lack of humanity, and absolute power exerted on our working bodies.

Stained hands

The strawberries for the cannery market were picked without the calyx, the crown and white part of the strawberry. Pickers would hold the berry with the thumb, index, and middle finger and squeeze the calyx out before throwing the juicy fruit in the plastic container. When the 24-pound container filled up, we would lift it up, put it on our shoulders, and walk to the end of the field. While we walked, copious amounts of red juice would fall all over our shoulders and backs. Our clothing would be covered in red stains. The first week of the cannery harvest, I picked 20 or 25 containers, between 480 and 600 pounds, every day. I was brutally exhausted at the end of the day!

Unlike other sharecropping women, I did not like wearing gloves to pick strawberries because these would slow me down. As a result, I would always have dark or red stains on my hands even after I washed my hands. When I was working, I did not like touching my face or my hair with my dirty hands. I always wore a red Mexican handkerchief to tighten my hair underneath a baseball hat. My baseball hat would cover my round face from the sun, but I would get burns from the wind. I would also wear a blouse with long sleeves or a sweatshirt to protect my arms from the sun, wind, and cold. On hot summer days, I would tie my blouse around my waist to cover my back. At the second-hand store, or in the swap meet, I would purchase tennis shoes, even if they had someone else's foot imprint. Nonetheless, these shoes were good to walk in the muddy strawberry fields. As a poor farm worker toiling under harsh conditions, I sought to protect my racialized, immigrant, fractured body.

At the end of the working day, my mom would tell me to go to the supermarket to buy groceries for dinner or lunch the next day. I was very embarrassed to go because I felt, and literally was, so dirty. With my red stained blouse and old shoes, I felt that I was symbolically coming from a bloody battlefield. When I had the shopping cart full with my mom's shopping list, I would walk to the women at the cash register. When paying, I would try to hide my dirty hands! The white women would take the money without touching my hands. I felt terrible, as if I was carrying a contagious disease. Usually, people would gaze at me at the store because I was sweaty and muddy. I would get angry at my mother for sending me to the store after work. She would say with dignity, "There is nothing wrong with working in the fields." This experience of going to the marketplace in California was devoid of social and emotional relations of the *tianguis* in Oaxaca. Every day after work, I yearned to return to my beloved Putla and México.

After working all day in the strawberry fields, my family engaged in rebuilding our sense of *comunalidad*. I remember with love that the entire family would sit in the living room to regain our humanity by watching television. We would watch baseball games because Fernando Valenzuela, from Sonora, México, was the pitcher for the Dodgers in the early 1980s. We loved Fernando! We felt so proud that such a young Mexican man was playing in a famous baseball team in Los Angeles. It did not matter how tired we felt, we did not miss the games during the season. We also watched soccer and basketball games. I loved seeing my favorite Black player, Magic Johnson, playing basketball with the Los Angeles Lakers. My family would sit to watch games, but my mind wandered. I felt so helpless in my life working as a farm worker. I did not think that I would have the energy or the physical strength to bear such brutal working days. I remember thinking I was going to die in those fields.

One day, I purchased an old short-wave radio in the swap meet. Every night before I went to sleep, I would listen to my favorite radio station, Radio Havana, which broadcasted from Havana, Cuba. I would close my eyes and imagine my friend and teacher Héctor demonstrating in front of the American embassy in México City. Sometimes, I would have a difficult time with the short-wave reception, and would struggle to find Radio Havana. Instead, I would find Voice of America broadcasting conservative programs. To make my life bearable, I would listen to la Trova

Cubana, Silvio Rodriguez or Pablo Milanes' songs, to lift my spirits. I took refuge in music as a source of inspiration and hope for a better future. In this manner, I rejected racial, patriarchal capitalist's dehumanization of my commoditized body, my fractured life, and super-exploitation. I sought to preserve my human dignity.

Mexican immigrant *rancheros*

Global corporations dominate the production of strawberries for the fresh and cannery markets in Spain, Morocco, México, Chile, Uruguay, Argentina, and the United States. California Giant, Sunrise, Reiter Affiliated Companies, and Driscoll grow berries in Central Florida, North Carolina, Georgia, Michigan, Oregon, Washington, and British Columbia in the United States. Strawberry fields evoke a romantic setting, but it is a carefully planned industrial setting of high-tech berry fields devoid of workers' living labor. California coastal regions such as Watsonville, Oxnard, and Santa Marta are production regions par excellence. Some corporations, such as Smackers and Dole, purchase strawberries for industrial processing of jelly or ice cream. Global investors farm strawberries in the Santa Marta Valley too.

In Santa Marta, California, the lucrative production of strawberries requires an extremely sophisticated and state-of-the-art infrastructure to post-handle a highly perishable commodity. Cooling plants are multi-million-dollar hubs that have special refrigerated areas to extend the post-harvest life of perishable fruits, and vegetables, shipped to national and global consuming markets. Each cooling plant has marketing centers selling millions of Californian hand-picked strawberries. Some cooling plants specialize in processing strawberries for jam, ice cream, and other industrialized consumption forms. Cooling plants handle millions of pounds of strawberries for the fresh and cannery global markets which Mexican immigrant hands, documented or undocumented, pick in the fields. The economic success of the strawberry industry is continuously heralded in the local news, yet farm workers are invisible.

A few Mexican immigrants, who were former sharecroppers in the strawberry industry, achieved socio-economic mobility by becoming independent *rancheros*. In the early 1980s, Mexican immigrants increased the size of their strawberry farms by having their own Mexican sharecroppers. Within a short period of time, a few Mexican *rancheros* became partners of transnational corporations operating in the Santa Marta Valley. For instance, Narciso López came to be a partner of Wal-Mart multinational corporation that was buying strawberries locally. Other Mexican immigrants achieved socio-economic mobility by farming a cornucopia of fruits and vegetables and providing fumigation services to undercapitalized Mexican family farmers. By the 1990s, a handful of Mexican immigrants achieved socio-economic mobility by farming hundreds of acres of strawberries, and vegetables, in the valley.

Some Mexican *rancheros* successfully built multi-million-dollar *culers* to handle the post-harvest of perishable fruits like strawberries and vegetables en route to global consuming markets. Because the strawberry is a fruit that has a very high metabolic rate, it starts to decay right after being picked on the fields. Farm workers must carefully handpick the fruit to avoid damaging it.

Therefore, farmers frequently deliver strawberry loads to cooling facilities because a single damaged fruit placed inside a marketing tray causes others to decay rapidly. High tech is employed to handle strawberries by manipulating oxygen reduction and carbon dioxide, which is injected on the pallets to prevent the fruit from aging. The adoption of high tech in the cooling centers stands in sharp contradiction with the foreign bodies, and hands, skillfully picking strawberries in the fields.

Deudas (debts)

Many relatively poor Mexican immigrants became family farmers borrowing large quantities of capital to produce strawberries in Santa Marta. In the mid-1980s, my father Pedro rented six acres of land from an old landowner, borrowed about $3,000 dollars per acre from the cooling plant, and invested $1,500 per acre of his own money. My father also had a loan, about $1,500 per acre, from the industrialized cooling plant. In addition, the fumigation company fumigated his farm by giving him credit to be paid during the harvest. Like most Mexican immigrant family farmers, Pedro had to amass approximately $6,000 per acre just to establish the strawberry farm. My father Pedro purchased on credit thousands of packaging supplies such as boxes and wires from *culers*. All of these loans and credit lines were repaid during the harvest when family farmers turned in the strawberry harvest for cooling plants to sell in global markets. Thus, cooling plants and fumigation companies facilitated the financialization of poor Mexican immigrant family farmers who entered into asymmetrical credit/debit relations of unregulated neoliberal economic markets that were not beneficial or ethical.

Family farmer Maria and José. Photo taken by author circa 2004.

Mexican immigrant family farmers produced strawberries for fresh and cannery global consuming markets. In good years, Pedro paid his short-term loans, their workers, and had profits. He usually reinvested profits in the farm (increasing acreage) or used them to recapitalize by buying old machinery for the farming operations. However, as globalization glutted consuming markets, strawberries were frequently dumped in the world market. In other words, global market prices precipitously fell because there was an oversupply of strawberries. My undercapitalized father Pedro and my two older brothers, who were also farming strawberries, owed so much money that they could not sleep at night. In a conversation, my older brother Andrés said that he "could not even buy milk for his children"!

Although cooling plants controlled the marketing and financing of strawberries, they did not assume any losses. Instead, cooling plants would recover their loans regardless of market prices, leaving many cash-strapped farmers without funds. Because cooling plants would automatically deduct their weekly payments, family farmers would receive very little each week. In many instances, Mexican immigrant family farmers did not receive a personal paycheck to support their families because paying wages to workers and loans to cooling plants took all their capital. In many instances, they paid wages with a check that did not have funds in the bank. Many times, my father Pedro and brothers did not receive a paycheck in order to pay their workers. To survive, and assuming his ethical responsibility with our countrymen, Pedro would borrow short-term loans from other Oaxaqueño friends living in northern California.

When my father became a family farmer in the strawberry industry, we would frequently visit our lifelong friends living in Healdsburg, California. Petra González, who was our neighbor in Putla, came to Healdsburg in the early 1970s. Before we migrated to México City, she and her children emigrated to Healdsburg. When there was a wedding, birthday, or any celebration in Petra's family, we would be invited to the party. We would visit them to camp next to the river which crossed in the vineyard where some of Petra's relatives worked. We would spend days swimming, eating, and catching up while sitting on the edge of the river. The river in Healdsburg brought memories of our beloved homeland, and we enjoyed our time together. We resisted social and cultural alienation by rebuilding our sense of *comunalidad* as we lived in a foreign land.

With every visit, we would bring them several boxes of fresh delicious strawberries. Prior to our departure, we would hand-pick the biggest, glossiest red strawberries to be eaten fresh. Sometimes, we would pick strawberries with long stems, which would be considered special. The strawberries with a stem would only be picked around Mother's Day and were generally special marketing orders. We would pick these strawberries for our friends who were (and are) very dear and special to us. My mother would cook strawberry jelly and can it in big bottles. We would occasionally bring them canned strawberry jelly, and they would give us grapes and bottles of the best wine. Despite the years and the physical separation, we lived in *comunalidad* together!

My mother in the family farm. Photo taken by author circa 2004

Once, I saw my father giving money to Petra's son Arturo. I asked my mother about it since I did not know the reason. She explained that Arturo had lent approximately $10,000 to my father, so he could pay the workers' salaries. Arturo, who was a tractor driver in a vineyard, saved money from work. When my father asked him for a short-term loan, he agreed, and he did not charge an interest rate. Nonetheless, my father paid back the loan and added a small gratuity for the friendly gesture. Without the emergency loan, my father would have not been able to pay his strawberry farm workers.

Global corporations transferred production risks to relatively poor Mexican immigrant farmers while they concentrated in the most profitable part of the global chain (loans, selling materials, and marketing). They banked on the sensibilities of a communal, respectable, and responsible Oaxaqueño man farming an expensive commodity that did not turn out to be a good business adventure in California. After several years of surviving market gluts, price swings, borrowing money, and asymmetrical power relations, my brothers Alfredo and Andrés became general farm supervisors while my parents Pedro and Guilla retired from farming strawberries. My sisters and I went to school, leaving agriculture.

Nurturing *comunalidad*

Mexican immigrant farm workers live, however, in poor enclaves found throughout the Santa Marta Valley. Prior to the arrival of Guilla's children from México in 1980, she and her husband lived in a small, but very cheap, rental unit called White Houses, which was located near the middle-class neighborhood of Orcutt, California. Guilla's youngest daughter, Queta, remembers that she was very happy when she arrived at White Houses from México

City in 1980. She was thinking that the family was finally going to be together for the first time in her life. As a fractured child, she said that she felt very, very happy. However, Guilla's family could not live in White Houses because the apartment was too small for all of them. Out of necessity, Guilla told Pedro to purchase a house with the money from her accident in the chili harvest in Santa Marta. A Puerto Rican family owned the house which was located on the western side of the Santa Marta Valley in a diverse *barrio* populated by white, Mexican Americans, and Puerto Rican people. However, the western side of the Santa Marta Valley became a Mexican *barrio* in a short period of time.

When my parents applied for a home loan to the bank, they did not qualify for the loan. My brother Andrés, who was working full time in the fields, was then added to the loan application, facilitating the purchasing of the house. My mother remembers that the house owner, a Puerto Rican man, was instrumental in the purchasing of the house because they did not know anything about owning a house in California. He advised them through the loan and escrow process. Like other houses in the western side of Santa Marta, the house had a master bedroom, two more bedrooms, a living room, and kitchen with a small dining space. My mother liked the house because it had a beautiful backyard with lemon and peach trees. Most importantly, owning a house was very important for the immigrant family because it allowed reunification of family members. The house became a powerful symbolic place to rebuild our sense of *comunalidad* (identity and belonging) as negated foreigners.

My mother's household would later accommodate more people as many friends, *compadres*, and countrymen came to work in

Santa Marta during the spring and summer time. Most of the visitors were men ranging in age between 18 and 50 years, and some women between the ages of 30 and 45 years. For a few years, Guilla's sister-in-law, and two of her daughters, also came to her house. Like many other farm-working families in the Santa Marta Valley, there were times when up to 30 people lived in the same house. Some would share a bedroom, others would sleep in the living room, and still others would stay in the garage. The humble house was definitely a very small place for so many Oaxaqueños living under extremely overcrowded conditions. These were the conditions that Major Smith denounced as the "Mexican problem". That is, poor immigrant and migrant farm workers living in overcrowded conditions while they work, documented or undocumented, in multi-million-dollar industries like strawberries. My parents sustained the social reproduction of these farm workers in Santa Marta since they did not pay rent or household bills. In doing this, their sense of *comunalidad*, an obligation and responsibility, subsidized agribusiness.

Today, my mother is a 90-year-old retired farm worker woman with an injured leg who spends her time cultivating Oaxa-California in the backyard of her poor enclave. Many years ago, my parents brought from Putla a *yerba santa* plant which they cultivat to condiment the traditional *pozole* Oaxaqueño. When my father Pedro was alive, he would take special care of it. For instance, he would build a shade with old wood and clothes to protect the tropical plant from cold mornings in winter. In fact, many Oaxaqueño families came to ask for leaves for their tasty *pozole*. Some would try to buy the leaves, but my mother would not charge a fee. Underneath the *yerba santa*, my mother placed orchid plants to cover them from the sun. In addition, my parents brought from our home town a seed of *capulines*. They carefully germinated it and planted the tree in their front yard. My mother cultivates yellow and pink roses, orchids, calla lilies, peaches, and lemon trees as well as a dragon fruit plant in her backyard. She has a favorite bush that has a tied green canopy full of purple flowers. In this tree, dozens of small birds build their nests as they hide from preying falcons. In the middle of the day in spring, the tree blooms with life! Every day, my mother fills plastic containers with fresh water and feeds the birds.

After germinating seeds from a *chirimoya* fruit that I purchased in the farmers market, I gifted my mom the baby tree. After four years, the *chirimoya* tree bore fruit. My mother harvests and distributes the *chirimoya* among all of her children and grandchildren. "… *Las manos de mi madre llegan al patio desde temprano*" (my mother's hands arrive at the patio at dawn) sings Mercedes Sosa in her song, a tribute to women's working hands. My mother's immigrant hands have always been busy building a piece of Oaxa-California in her backyard. In doing this, she is powerfully rebuilding belonging, fractured identity, and place.

Last year my mother purchased a *chayote* shrub, a Mesoamerican staple squash, and she planted it in her backyard. She tied the *chayote* sprouts to a thread so the branches would grow on the clothesline. Now, the *chayote* plant has approximately eight *chayotes* hanging from the cloth line. I like to eat baby *chayotes*, but my mother does not like them. One day, I said to my mother, "Mama, can I cut a baby *chayote*?" She replied, "No, wait one more week." I tried to convince her that the best *chayotes* are the baby ones, but to no avail. The next week, I asked my mother to give me a baby *chayote*, as my mouth was watering, but she did not allow me to cut it until it was large and fully mature. One day, my mother's neighbor told her to water the plant and to add support to the *chayote* plant because it has many baby *chayotes*. The plant will break or die if it is not well taken care of. My mother agrees with him, but she plants the *chayote*, like the tomatoes, to efficiently consume the lawn's water. When the *chayotes* were mature, she gave me one! I resisted my "Otherness", as a negated and despised Mexican/Oaxaqueña immigrant, when I ate Mesoamerican staple foods. In a powerful symbolic way, I rebuilt my identity rooted in a sense of *comunalidad*, dignity, belonging, culture, and history by consuming Mesoamerican fruits and comfort foods.

As a retired farm worker, my mother lives in the same home in the western part of the Santa Marta Valley. She is now 90 years old and has difficulty walking. She has a knee that is bent inward, impeding her normal walk. Her back hurts when she sits for long periods of time. With the support of her cane stick, she walks in the neighborhood picking up tin cans. When she has three or four full trash bags, she uploads them to her Ford pickup truck and takes them to the recycling center where she receives a few dollars in payment. With the sale of her recycling bottles, she complements her meager retirement check. My mother is an extremely poor retiree who lives alone in her house. However, she always has a pot of sweet *calabaza* and *chayotes* for her sons and daughters who visit. She rekindles her *communalidad* and the love for her children keeps her alive in a foreign land.

Conclusion

My multigenerational family's labor history reveals the struggle of living labor in the production of perishable lucrative farm commodities. During the Bracero Program, my grandfather and father became full-time migrant wage workers in California while their families stayed back in Oaxaca and México City. In the post-Bracero era, my mother became a migrant farm worker as she traveled with my father to agricultural regions where she saw families with children harvesting fresh commodities. She painfully saw her own children picking strawberries for sybarite world consumers who demanded perfect commodities. In California, we struggled to retain our negated existence, and my mother fought legally, as poor immigrant farm workers toiling for wages, or non-wages, in an agriculture without ethical values. I was incorporated in a sharecropping family that complemented its poor livelihood with the wage and non-wage labor of young and old members.

Globalization, however, changed the social relations of production as Mexican immigrants achieved socio-economic mobility as *rancheros* and family farmers in the strawberry industry. My father became a relatively poor family farmer who struggled to succeed in the world market. After a few years, my parents retired from farming strawberries in California and my sisters and I left agriculture to attend city college and university.

With time the global demand for strawberries was easily met with the development of a state-of-the-art infrastructure to market millions of boxes of handpicked strawberries for global consumers in sharp contrast to the neglected working-class *barrios* of Santa Marta. My family's living labor sustained their resistance, from an exteriority or outside of the system, and my mother maintains her own and the family's identity by planting Mexican staples in her own backyard. Our sense of *comunalidad* has grown and even expanded as my late father and mother strengthen it every day.

4
Education and
la facultad negada

I was sitting at the dining table after picking strawberries all day, when I heard a polite knock on the door. I suspected it was Mormon missionaries who would frequently knock on the door, and after the long day I did not feel like having a conversation. My younger sister opened the door to a woman who introduced herself as a Chicana, bilingual, retired teacher named Mary Ellen. In a soft tone, Mary Ellen asked in Spanish, "Is there anyone who wants to learn English?" Although I had begun to learn English words on my own, I struggled with grammatical principles. I could not believe my luck! Mary Ellen, who was intimately familiar with white educational oppression, quietly subverted racial patriarchal domination of Mexican immigrant people. She changed my life by presenting the idea of studying and learning in a different cultural milieu. Over the course of many years, I developed my education, or *facultad*, to understand my family and my own neoliberal working-class history.

Chicana writer Gloria Anzaldúa (1987) mentioned in her book *La Frontera: The New Mestiza* the concept of *la facultad*, which she defined as the ability to understand the world through sensibility, emotions like fear and pain, awareness, and perceptions.

Among Chicanas living in the borderlands, *la facultad* represented the capacity to recognize multiple forms of cultural and sexual oppression. *La facultad* became a profound sense of awareness such that it shifted the perception of "objects and people" (Anzaldúa, 1987, p. 61). *La facultad* was so powerful that it became almost like another sense, with the capacity to grow in moments of crisis. For Indigenous Bolivian philosopher Rafael Bautista (2014), "La facultad [was] the power of life, of wanting to avoid death, of push[ing] forward" (p. 73). From this perspective, *la facultad* could be like an energy that could fabricate an alternative for a better future. *La facultad* is a "metanarrative" of Mexican immigrant education "at the level of experience" (Givens, 2021, pp. 8–11). Rooted in my sense of *comunalidad*, my *facultad* produced an awareness, consciousness, emotions, and energy to confront multiple forms of oppression and aggression in the world of academia. In other words, *la facultad* allows me to reflect about a particular moment, or conjuncture, in my life when I hoped to become an instructor in the public university system.

I developed *la facultad* by learning English as a Second Language, attending university, and graduating successfully with a doctoral degree in Cultural Anthropology from California's public university system. My *facultad* was rejected by nonprofit organizations, and it was negated by the UC *Tres Calmecac's* Chicana and Chicano Studies Department and white institutions in academia. After an existential crisis, I found strength and sensibilities in my sense of *comunalidad* such that I regained my *facultad* in becoming a public intellectual.

In the section, Negating my *facultad*, I narrated having an existential crisis. The reader may want to skip this section or proceed with caution.

Developing my *facultad*

I developed my *facultad* hoping to change the path of my fractured immigrant life from 1981 to 1999. While I worked on my parents' sharecropping plot, I felt nauseated with the sweet aroma of freshly picked strawberries, and I did not like eating the perfectly conical, shining, red strawberries. Oftentimes, I thought the strawberries were killing me and turning me into a quadruped mammal, work-machine, *caballito*. I remember that many farm workers listened to music in Spanish while they weeded out cauliflower or picked strawberries. I recall that most radio stations played *ranchero* music which I associated with *cantinas* in México City. I did not like the popular Mexican singer Vicente Fernandez, Los Tigres del Norte, or Mariachi music because I grew up listening to radio stations playing romantic music from México City. To avoid listening to other people's radios, I purchased a small portable radio that fit in my pocket. I would listen to radio stations that played country music while picking strawberries. I liked Loretta Lynn only because I could clearly hear the lyrics of her songs. I could not connect emotionally with country music as I did in Spanish; however, I could distinguish the words in English.

I did not like going to the grocery store not knowing what people said to me. I felt there was no empathy for my lack of communication skills and people did not listen to me. To break the silence, I began to memorize a verb per day: *walk, swim, pick*. I also carried my small bilingual dictionary in my handbag. Like the grocery shopping list that my mom gave me as a child, I easily memorized words in English. Slowly, I began to build my own vocabulary in English. Every night, after work, I would take a piece of paper and write each verb seven times in the present or past tense. Then, I built short sentences conjugating the verb using different tenses:

> *I walked in the park* ~ past tense.
> *My butt hurts when I shit* ~ present tense.
> *I will not pick strawberries every day!* ~ future tense.

I felt that lack of language skills placed me in the zone of nonbeing, in a sterile, dehumanized place. I felt that my fractured existence was invisible or negated in society. I was simply not seen, nor was I heard. This was a very scary feeling.

On the day when the Chicana teacher knocked on my door, I raised my hand without thinking twice about it. My younger sister said, me too. I could see the teacher's brown eyes shining with delight. The next few months, Mary Ellen came to our home to teach English to my younger sister and me. Mary Ellen brought back an idea and the dream to study and learn. Mary Ellen, a compassionate, retired, bilingual, Chicana teacher, did not need a political program to break the immigrant community's silence and language, exclusion, and oppression. My mother was also telling us to go to school. I began to break the cultural alienation in which I was living as a young Mexican immigrant woman, uprooted from the *comunalidad* in Oaxaca.

To avoid paying state fees in the city college, I eagerly waited a year to enroll in the community college. In 1981, I enrolled in English as a Second Language (ESL) in the local community college program. Two years after my arrival in Santa Marta, I went to night school after work. Many ESL classes were taught by the bilingual teacher, Mr. Pérez. His students were primarily Mexican *rancheros* learning English in the college. I also met other women from the central Mexican states of Michoacán, Guanajuato, and Jalisco.

I remember Mr. Pérez would kneel in front of me telling me, *fíjate en mi lengua. Pongo la lengua entre los dientes para pronunciar la "th" en Inglés* (observe my tongue. I placed it between my teeth to pronounce the "th" in English). He would tell us: *tienen que aprender grafemas y fonemas* (you must learn graphemes and morphemes). For example, "work" (w-o-r-k) has four graphemes or small units of sound, and morphemes like "in [or] ing" or words that cannot be divided. I was always impressed by the passion with which Mr. Pérez taught English to his farm worker students. I dreamt of becoming an excellent and compassionate instructor just like Mr. Perez or my old teacher Héctor who employed "affective epistemologies" in the classroom (Givens, 2021, p. 8). These teachers loved the art of teaching and learning.

I then enrolled in regular courses at the local community college during the day. My older brother told me to enroll in math courses for which I did not need much English. The numbers were the same in English or Spanish, said my wise older brother, the engineer, with whom I played marbles in my homeland.

But I loved reading and enrolled in all of the sociology courses offered by the city college, and quickly befriended a few Mexican immigrants who were also bilingual students. They would tell me which courses to enroll in if I wanted to transfer to the University of California or the Polytechnic. In the 1960s, Native American, Black, and Chicano Civil Rights activists demanded an opportunity to get an education and I benefited from it. My friends and I believed that we would have many professional opportunities by getting an education. My wounded, fractured body began to dream of changing the social order of society.

My Mexican friends played an important role in the development of my *facultad* in the community college. They would tell me to speak to the bilingual counselors in the college so that I could plan my courses. I did not want to speak to the counselors, but my friends insisted. I gathered the courage to speak to the Chicana counselor, who advised me not to apply to the university. My older sister would ask me, "Why not?" My older sister Maribel, who studied anthropology at the National Institute of Anthropology and History in México City, would tell me *aquí y en China, estudiar, es lo mismo* (In China and here, studying is the same). She convinced me that I would succeed as a student. I did not listen to the community counselor when I applied to UC *Tres Calmecac* (UCTC) under the Affirmative Action Program. In 1985, UCTC accepted my application to study sociology. While I lived in México City, I wanted to study medicine. However, California's strawberry fields reshaped my educational dream, and I wanted to study sociology or the social reasons for such a drastic change.

I recall that I was afraid to attend the university. Even though I could read a lot of English, I could not write or speak well. Besides, I was a non-traditional, fractured working-class woman, Mexican immigrant, an ESL speaker and writer, and older (by three to five years) than most undergraduate students at the university. I was aware of the new situation. These were fears or vulnerabilities that I had to overcome in order to study sociology. My friends in the community college did not go to the university, some got married while others went into business. I leaned on my radical pedagogies, knowledge and discipline, and persever-ance to study at the university.

In my first quarter at UCTC, I registered in a sociology class where I wrote an individual research paper about Zapotec (Oaxaca) cul-ture. At the end of the fall quarter in 1985, the professor returned my research paper with a note apologizing because his cat peed on my term paper! He also spilled coffee on my term paper. I did not care about the cat peeing or the spilled coffee on my term paper at all. When I received my paper, I was very happy to have obtained a B grade on my research paper. I still have the term paper in a box because it was the first test of my ability, or my *facultad*, to study in English. After I received my grade, I knew that I could really make it in school. My *facultad* became the driv-ing force to uplift myself through an education.

In an upper division sociology class, I met a Chicano bilingual student named Samuel who liked to sit next to me. He would frequently whisper in my ear: *¡Estoy ciego! ¡Tanta blancura me deslumbra!* (I am blind! So much whiteness blinds me!). I would smile at him because I did not understand his blindness. It took

me a while to realize that he was referring to his racialized experiences in classes dominated by white, middle-class students.
Like me, he had been admitted to UCTC through the Affirmative
Action Program. Samuel and I had so much in common as I too
felt blinded in sociology. I made political speeches in the public
buses in México City, yet I sat quietly in class to not draw attention from the teaching assistants and professors. I was afraid to
participate in class because white students would laugh at my
Mexican accent. Soon, I realized that speaking English with a
working-class accent did not bring me whiteness, status, power,
or prestige.

My friend Samuel enrolled in a class taught by a Mexican anthropologist who was doing ethnographic research in the Santa
Marta Valley. Samuel had spoken to him about me, and the professor, Pablo Arizmendi, wanted to talk to me. I was afraid to talk to
the professor so I ignored my friend's recommendation to meet
with him. Samuel continued to insist that I visited him during
his office hours in the Anthropology Department, but I ignored
him. With my permission, Professor Arizmendi called me on the
phone to tell me he was visiting Santa Marta. He wanted to meet
with me to explain his research project in the area. We met in
a Mexican restaurant in Santa Marta for over two hours. At the
end of the meeting, I was very impressed by his interest in poor,
Mexican, immigrant, neoliberal farm workers in California. After
I met Arizmendi, I declared Cultural Anthropology as my minor.

Professor Arizmendi, who became the Director of the Chicano
Research Center, hired me to do ethnographic research among
Mexican immigrant sharecroppers in Santa Marta. During the
summer of 1988, I interviewed Mexican immigrant sharecroppers

from the states of Michoacán, Guanajuato, Jalisco, and my family from Oaxaca. Each time, I would carefully write my research notes on my ethnographic journal and Arizmendi would review them. Usually, he would give me feedback on how to improve my notes. He would ask questions to help me build case studies. I recall that he spent hours explaining ethnographic field methods and how to improve ethnographic notes. In December of 1988, I obtained my bachelor's degree in Sociology and my minor in Cultural Anthropology. One day, Professor Arizmendi invited me to apply to graduate school in the Anthropology Department.

I applied to the terminal master's program in Cultural Anthropology at UC *Tres Calmecac* in 1989. I knew that I could do research among Mexican immigrant farmers and farm workers in Santa Marta. I wanted to understand the reasons, forces, and structures that shaped my own fragmented immigrant life. Besides, I felt that I could work with Arizmendi and that he would successfully mentor my *facultad*.

Although I could not write English well, Arizmendi never had any doubts about my intellectual capacity to succeed in the master's program. He understood that I was part of the Oaxaqueño, and Mexican, immigrant community who created wealth by planting, cultivating, and harvesting rather expensive commodities that sybarite consumers desired all over the world. As a cultural anthropologist, he was studying huge social transformations such as the demographic shift occurring in the state of California where thousands of Mexican immigrant families were settling in rural communities. As an engaged scholar, Professor Arizmendi worked hard building the Mexican immigrant and Chicano community's *facultad*, most especially, my own *facultad*. In the summer of 1990, more or less, I did research in Arvin, California, to document the presence of Mexican Indigenous migrant workers from a small town near Putla, Oaxaca. I employed this research to write my master's thesis in Cultural Anthropology, after which I applied to the doctoral program in 1991.

I remember that I enrolled in graduate courses taught by professors specializing in Africa and Latin America. I had the opportunity to learn about South African peasant households, and shanty towns in Peru. However, my favorite classes were on the ethnology of peasant societies in México and rural communities in California. As a graduate student, I chose to study with Professor Arizmendi who later supervised my ethnographic doctoral research among Mexican immigrant family farmers and *rancheros* in Santa Marta, California. Unlike many of my friends studying far away cultures, I wanted to understand the persistence of family farming in an advanced agrarian capitalist economy.

I framed my doctoral research hypothesis to study Karl Marx's (1961) prediction of the disappearance of family farming with the development of capitalism. I also designed the research methodology using participant-observation, open-ended interviews, collecting genealogies, and life and health histories. From June of 1993 to September of 1994, I spent hours participating and observing the production of strawberries, interviewing family farms, farm workers, truck drivers, bankers, and specialized technical personnel (like fumigators, pest control advisors, supervisors). I also gathered genealogies (mapping family histories) to understand migration, settlement, and the role of Mexican immigrant labor in agriculture. Based on my ethnographic research and my experience, I found that family non-wage labor was the key for family farming survival in an advanced capitalist economy.

After I completed my ethnographic research, my husband and I relocated to Pamplona, Spain, from 1995 to 1999. With a baby son in tow, I wrote some chapters of my dissertation while living in Pamplona. In January of 2000, I returned to California with my family. I kept writing multiple drafts, one chapter at a time.

I recall that I was determined to complete my doctoral dissertation in Cultural Anthropology, for which I had the support of Professor Arizmendi. I would write a chapter of the dissertation and I would give it to him. After he would carefully read it, we would meet to discuss his feedback. I still have all of his comments about my doctoral dissertation. Recently, I found a note he wrote in one of my journals:

Guille:
Ya leí la Introducción. Buscame como a la 1:30 para revisarla juntos. P.A.

(Guille: I read the Introduction. Find me around 1:30 to review it together. P.A.)

In 2002, I finished my doctoral degree in Cultural Anthropology from UC *Tres Calmecac* after which I applied for jobs in academia, but I was not offered a job. As explained in the next section, I worked in the nonprofit sector for a few years. Throughout this time, I heard a small voice in my ear whispering, become a teacher. Teaching became my dream.

Almost a decade after I completed my doctoral dissertation, I became an adjunct professor at UC *Tres Calmecac*. Professor

Pablo Arizmendi became the Interim Chair of the Department of Chicano Studies at UC *Tres Calmecac*, and he hired several Mexican and Chicano Visiting Professors. In 2009, he offered me to teach undergraduate courses and I did not think twice about such an amazing opportunity. Professor Arizmendi negotiated with the Dean of Social Sciences so that I could teach five upper division courses and dedicate some time (33 percent or the equivalent to one course per quarter) to train undergraduate students. I became a full-time Adjunct Professor teaching assigned courses on Mexican and Chicano farm labor history, culture, and social movements while I trained Mexican immigrant and Chicano undergraduate students to do ethnographic research.

I recall teaching a course called Body, Culture, and Power that I developed to explore the politics of Chicano identity in relation to foodways and sexuality. This class included reading material on *quinceañeras* to understand coming-of-age body rituals and sexuality in the Chicana and Mexican culture. I added readings by Chicana anthropologists like Norma Cantú and José Limón, and feminist scholar Cherri Moraga. I incorporated music and literature as the course evolved over a few years. Because many of my female Chicana and Mexican students had celebrated their *quinceañeras*, they loved reading about the ritual. Using a pedagogy of freedom, I required an autoethnographic journal for students to reflect on readings and their own stories with Body, Culture, and Power. At the end, a feminist perspective enriched the course to the extent that it was offered every quarter. My teaching evaluations were excellent and I truly loved teaching this class. I shared my knowledge and I was very happy!

In Chicano Studies, I became a communal-oriented instructor developing with confidence all of my assignments around the concept of the Chicano community. Instead of individual exams, students wrote term papers in small groups of six to eight students. Most students would inevitably run into problems. Students could not agree on a meeting time, or they could not find common themes. I would assign team leaders to organize the schedule, to select the bibliography, and to coordinate meetings. I dedicated class time to organizing students in order to teach them the power of studying collectively, rather than as capitalist competitive individuals, in the classroom. I was determined not to reproduce structures of white power.

I also used the concept of community to bridge the gap between theory and praxis. Students would write their own stories about the United States-Mexican border, immigration, body and power, incarceration, and deportation of undocumented members of their immigrant families and communities. In other words, I felt successful training a new generation of Chicana/o scholars who would have the intellectual foundations to understand historical struggles, critique racial, patriarchal capitalism, and address systemic intersectional oppression. They had the capacity, the energy, and awareness to seek social change. They could develop their own *facultad*. I was so happy. I was so proud of my *facultad*! My families in California and México were proud of me too.

As part of my non-teaching time, I organized an ethnographic fieldwork project to train undergraduate students to do research among poor Mexican immigrant farm workers in Santa Marta. I recruited Mexican immigrant and Chicano undergraduate students from all of my courses in the department, and designed my course to teach Chicano history using Albert Camarillo's *Chicanos in a Changing Society: From Mexican Pueblos to American Barrios, 1848–1930*. This was an excellent introduction to my research project because it discussed Chicano local politics, racism, displacement, and working-class struggles to survive multiple forms of oppression. Furthermore, I compiled a series of ethnographic research articles while I used my own experience as a researcher in California. I also organized students to go to the strawberry fields in Santa Marta where they had the opportunity to interview farm workers. Since my older brothers were farm supervisors in the strawberry industry, they would allow me to visit their farms with my students. I was training students to see their communities with critical eyes. I felt that my *facultad* was truly blossoming in Chicano Studies such that I forgot about my fractured neoliberal existence. I did not have doubts about my capacity to succeed as an instructor. Aztlán became my new home.

A small group of undergraduate Chicano students began an ethnographic research project, called MILPA (Mexican Immigrant Labor and Producers Association), among Mexican immigrant family farmers in Santa Marta. They applied for a grant to a local foundation, interviewed family farmers, organized meetings, and created a cooperative to address the power of cooling plants in the Santa Marta Valley. This project was supported by the new Chicano Studies Institute's Director and by Professor Pablo Arizmendi. Under my supervision, the students wrote a social justice paper and presented their findings at the National Association of Chicana and Chicano Studies (NACCS) in Los Angeles. At the end, all the undergraduate students who participated in this ethnographic project applied successfully to graduate school. By recruiting, training, and mentoring Chicano students, I was providing a service to the community. In a sense, I replicated the models from which I was trained as an ethnographer. I was instrumental in helping my undergraduate students develop their *facultad*. I was a successful Affirmative Action beneficiary, albeit adjunct professor in the university.

Rejecting my *facultad*

Before I became an adjunct faculty, I worked in the nonprofit sector between 2004 and 2008. Because I could not find a teaching job, I applied for a job at the nonprofit organization that provided Head Start, a federal preschool program for poor children in Tres Rivers County, but I was very frustrated with being a caseworker. In 2005, a friend of mine who is a professor at Cal-State Grasshopper called me to tell me that a nonprofit was looking for an evaluator. My friend's wife, who had a master's degree in education, was working at the nonprofit as a Teacher Coordinator. I was thrilled at the opportunity.

I applied for the job and was quickly called for an interview in Grasshopper. My husband, my two children, and I drove to Grasshopper. When we stepped out of the vehicle after the three-hour drive, we were so hot. I was sweaty and exhausted, but deeply excited. I met the nonprofit Executive Director for the interview, and afterwards he called me and offered me the job. I was hired! Indeed, I was excited at the opportunity to work in one of the many UFW's nonprofit organizations in California. I thought of this as a path to retake my radical political life, which I missed so much. I thought that this was an excellent opportunity to work as an evaluator of farm worker adult educa-tion programs. I had built my *facultad* from the bottom up and I could share my knowledge working with poor immigrant neo-liberal farm workers. I considered this to be a unique opportunity to improve working conditions in the fields. I was confident in the power of my lived experience and *facultad*.

The Executive Director was one of the sons-in-law of farm worker leader César Chávez. Like hundreds of Mexican Americans, he joined the farm worker movement as a young man. At the height of the farm worker movement, there was an attempt to kill César Chávez, and he became Chávez's personal bodyguard. He would frequently stand guard in the homes or places where César Chávez slept. At public rallies, he would guard *su patrón* with his life. At that time, I was flabbergasted at a farm worker volunteer becoming an Executive Director of a nonprofit organization. As a student of Mexican and Chicana/o labor, I have seen photo-graphs of César Chávez, Helen Favela Chávez, Dolores Huerta, Marshall Ganz, but I have never seen my boss. Frank Bardacke (2012) briefly mentioned that my boss was part of the elite group purging dissidents in the United Farm Workers Union. Because I did not know his history in the farm worker movement or labor union, I admired the way a bodyguard had become such an important man, directing a nonprofit organization and manag-ing adult education programs for poor farm workers. This story was the embodiment of the American Dream from rags to riches.

The Executive Director had small classrooms in rural communi-ties throughout Kern County. Some of these classrooms were located in the back of small churches or shared space with pro-grams like Head Start. The nonprofit also offered several training programs like driving a forklift or tractors for farm workers to achieve socio-economic mobility in agriculture. In 2005, because the Director was planning to expand his services, he employed me to evaluate the programs. I was so excited, thinking that I had the perfect job!

My *facultad* could finally service the farm worker community that I so much loved. I thought that I could make so many contributions using the science of anthropology to improve the lives of poor farm workers in California. As a Cultural Anthropologist trained on qualitative methodologies, I employed a mixed range of methods like participant-observation, interviews, and case studies to assess the program's effectiveness. I even wrote my ethnographic notes in an electronic journal to easily share.

Two months after I started to work in the office, the Executive Director told me to help write a grant for the Ford Foundation. Several staff members had intensive sessions writing the grant that had a big evaluation piece. The Director employed a cadre of professional people, which included a year-round consultant with a doctoral degree in economics, an evaluation director/consultant, several bilingual teachers, one administrator, and an evaluation coordinator. The economist who was from Latin America directed the writing team. The Executive Director trusted him. I was very impressed with the professional team with which the Director surrounded himself in the office. I always wondered where the resources to pay such a professional cadre were coming from. I learned that the nonprofit was successful obtaining private grants to train farm workers. It also obtained federal grants and was working with local institutions to expand the farm working training programs.

I was a few months into my job when journalist Miriam Pawel (2006) published a series of articles in the *Los Angeles Times* criticizing the United Farm Workers Union. I knew that funding from foundations played an extremely important role in the life of the nonprofit organization where I was working. When Pawel was doing research, my boss opened up the financial books to her. Now, he felt betrayed by Miriam Pawel who accused the union of failing to pay income taxes, fraud, and nepotism among other serious accusations. Pawel's article was not surprising since we had spent so much time writing a grant for the Ford Foundation. I also recalled the Executive Director saying that he introduced Pawel to the top-ranking leader in the UFW.

Pawel's articles shook the internal leadership of the labor union, who were unhappy with the bad publicity. One of the leaders called for an emergency meeting at the UFW's headquarter office, Nuestra Señora de la Reina de la Paz, located in the Tehachapi mountains, in Keene, California. As employees of the nonprofit, the meeting was compulsory, so all the staff jumped into a car, and drove to La Reina. When we arrived at La Reina, I was left with my mouth open. This was such a beautiful place surrounded by pine trees, oaks, and a small stream. La Reina was located at the foot of the Tehachapi mountain, with an abundance of flora and fauna. I could hear birds chirping in the trees! What a spectacular place. I felt that I was in heaven. I could not avoid thinking about the sacrifice of farm workers walking miles and miles with bloody feet to reach the power house in Sacramento. La Reina stood in sharp contradiction to the class struggle of Mexican, Chicano, and Filipino farm workers!

As I stood in the crowd listening to the leader's speech, a co-worker whispered that Nuestra Señora de la Paz was César Chávez's personal retreat center. César Chávez, he said, would disappear for days, as he went on long walks in the forest. In the middle of the oaks and pine trees, César Chávez would smoke "weed". I uttered, really? I was embarrassed to tell my coworker to shut up so that I could hear the passionate speech.

The next few days, my boss spent hours on the phone talking to foundations that promised to continue supporting his farm worker programs despite Miriam Pawel's accusations of tax evasion. I remember thinking that the political commitment of foundations to continue the economic support avoided ethical, moral, and political questions. How could Pawel understand the power of farm workers or the sacrifices made by César and his family to give power to farm workers? Nuestra Señora de la Paz stood there in humility at the foot of a big mountain, surrounded by natural beauty, chirping birds, noble, peaceful, and powerful like César.

Two months after Pawel's publications, I gave my boss a report based on my evaluations, pointing out that all of the classrooms had many social problems. I documented the lack of communication between the Director, Coordinator, Teachers, and the students. Although the teachers would make a great effort in teaching ESL courses, they did not have any teaching experience, and some could not speak English well. Many times, the teachers did not have exams, keys to enter in the buildings, or students in the classroom. Students attended sporadically, did not qualify in some cases, or had many challenges. Some young women would bring their children to the classroom. Many teachers complained of the lack of supervision or lack of direct involvement from the Coordinator and the Director. In addition, I did not like that the Director planned to charge fees to farm workers. I remember reading the results of a survey: "How much could you pay to learn 20 hours of English as a Second Language?" As explained below, charging fees for a poorly executed ESL program was unjustified in my view. Grants were already paying for the training programs and I did not like the fee modality. In my professional opinion, the nonprofit was having a big problem bridging theory (bilingual education) and praxis (teaching English to farm workers with low levels of literacy). Nonetheless, I wrote a diplomatic Evaluation Summative Report because I feared the social consequences.

After I turned in the report to the Executive Director, I quickly realized that the Executive Director did not intend to assess the effectiveness of the farm worker programs in depth. The previous Evaluator had written questionnaires and score cards to evaluate the programs, so the results were always positive. This information was used to promote the farm worker training programs. I realized that the Director wanted to impress agribusiness partners signing training contracts with the nonprofit. Surveys would be conducted among 20 students. For me, the science of the surveys was highly questionable. The Director did not intend to have ethical evaluations of the farm working programs. In theory, the ESL program was very successful, yet the ESL training program was failing in practice.

I also recall that the Executive Director would have weekly staff meetings that began routinely with César Chávez's prayer. I did not know the prayer, nor was I Catholic. At every office meeting, I stood in complete silence, placing my right hand over my heart, remembering the Oath of Allegiance in the American Consulate office in the border town of Ciudad Juárez when I swore to be an American loyal citizen. Leading the César Chávez prayer, the Executive Director and my coworkers would say, "… let's remember those who have died for justice; for they have given us life …". This was a strange ritual to cultivate the saintly image of "Cezar", as he always pronounced César's name in English. I would look at Cezar's photograph in the office, and I would imagine my brother-in-law and his parents walking on the streets of Los Angeles chanting *si se puede!*

Before or after the prayer, the Executive Director would tell my co-worker Maria that she looked "very pretty". At times, he would tell her that she had very "pretty legs"! I was shocked the first time that I heard his sexist remarks. However, I was surprised that Maria did not stop him. One day, she told me that she hated him. I asked her, "Why don't you talk to the Chair of the UFW Board of Directors?" She replied, "All of them are family or very loyal friends." She also said that she would have many enemies. Instead of dealing with one sexist pig, she would have to confront the Chávez clan. Besides, she added, "the ED's wife worked for the labor union and she could terminate my fellowship". As a single, young Chicana mother, she could not afford to lose the economic support of her employer. She chose to endure the sexual harassment. I remember that I felt humiliated and powerless to confront the sexual harassment. However, I would frown every time that I heard a sexual comment. To express my disapproval, I would smack my lips!

In June of 2006, the Executive Director called me into his office. Dressed in his elegant suit, wearing a tie, and expensive black shoes, he told me that the nonprofit could no longer keep me on the payroll. I was shocked and could not say anything to him. When he gave me my last paycheck, I was trembling. I felt morally devastated for moving my entire family to Grasshopper, for which my husband had left a good job. A job that he loved and enjoyed very much. I felt terrible! My *facultad* stumbled.

After nine months of working in Grasshopper, I was disenchanted with the nonprofit world. I could not stand the sexual harassment, the pointless efforts, and failure of the ESL program.

I never spoke to anyone about my experience in this nonprofit because I felt ashamed. Shame was a powerful tool to silence my *facultad*. I was embarrassed for years because I took this as a personal failure. I was totally naïve, thinking that one of César Chávez's nonprofit could be a radical, non-capitalist enterprise at the service of poor farm workers. I could not avoid thinking that my *facultad* was negated for political reasons.

Negating my *facultad*

My *facultad* was systemically negated and assaulted by Eurocentric epistemologies and white institutions, between 2009 and 2017, prevalent in American academe. When Professor Pablo Arizmendi agreed to be the Interim Chair of the Chicano Studies Department at UC *Tres Calmecac*, he was responsible for hiring Adjunct Faculty as well as the new Chair. A well-known Chicana scholar, Maria Antoinette Gimenez, became the new Chair of the department. I remember that the department, the graduate students, and undergraduate students were very happy with her.

During her reign, she changed the name of the department from Chicano Studies to Chicana and Chicano Studies.

Maria Antoinette Gimenez soon fired all the temporary Adjunct and Visiting Professors working in the Chicana and Chicano Studies Department. I remember that I received a reduced paycheck. I asked the department's manager about it and she explained that the Chair had taken away the non-teaching time. Immediately, I made an appointment to speak to her in her office. At the meeting, Professor Gimenez said that I did not have publications. I still remember that she gave me numerous examples of how she sacrificed family gatherings like Thanksgiving or Christmas to work on her publications. In her Eurocentric colonized mind, she measured success based on the number of academic publications. I recall how she condescendingly remarked, "You do not even write commentaries?" I did not know what commentaries were about, or the reason for writing commentaries. Since I was an Adjunct Professor, I was preparing myself to become an instructor for which I did not need publications or to write commentaries. I thought that I was following the right course of action. I was an excellent instructor! Maria Antoinette was evaluating my performance based on the expectations of tenured track professors who taught fewer courses and had more resources than I did as an adjunct faculty. However, I did not contradict her false premise, fearing the consequences. Then, Maria Antoinette said outright that I needed to start looking for another job. The veiled condescending threat echoed in my mind for days and months!

A few months later, Maria Antoinette sent me an email announcing the termination of my adjunct position in the Chicana and

Chicano Studies Department. The email said that the department was going to hire two tenured track professors and that they were planning to dismiss me within a year. I was distraught and did not quite understand such a cold and deadly message. The email reflected my obliterated, negated, and despised *facultad*. In my desperation to retain my job, I wrote a letter appealing the decision of the department. I vividly remember that I invoked the spirit of the labor union in my letter. I thought that labor rights were part of the historical struggle of the Chicana and Chicano people and that the department would rethink the decision and honor my teaching contract. On March 19, 2013, when I received the email, my wounded neoliberal body shivered!

To my surprise, Maria Antoinette shared the email with two professors who were part of the Undergraduate Committee in the department. No one bothered to answer my letter. With the assistance of the lecturers' labor union, I filed a grievance against the Chicana and Chicano Studies Department. These Chicana professors just ignored my letter and my grievance. I could not run home and tell my father about the attacks on my faculty position. Nevertheless, I shared my problems with my older sister, who would tell me: why are you surprised? *¡Las Chicanas son asi!* (Chicanas are like that). I was blinded once more. My heart was broken!

I immediately resumed my search for academic jobs after the Chair of Chicana and Chicano Studies told me her plan to terminate my employment. Because I was a firm believer in the public university system, I sent job applications to public community colleges and universities targeting Chicano Studies and Cultural Anthropology departments. I recall that I applied to UC Irvine where the department was looking for a Cultural Anthropologist. Most of the time, I applied to many public universities like Cal-State San Marcos and Cal-State Los Angeles because I wanted to share my knowledge as an instructor. Due to the demographic shift in California, the Cal-State system was increasing its Mexican immigrant and first college-going generation in their campuses. I thought that I was a perfect fit for their departments.

I applied for a Latino scholar position in the Universal Studies Department at San Luis Obispo (SLO), which is part of the California Polytechnic State University system. I was extremely happy when Cal-State invited me to the job interview. I felt that I had a unique opportunity in a university that had a big agricultural and hands-on orientation. I thought that I could work closer to home, do research in my area, and be closer to my family. I had worked on developing my *facultad* for years, and I felt prepared theoretically and empirically for the endeavor. I was so hopeful and excited at the opportunity to become an instructor. This was the perfect opportunity to slam the door in the face of many people.

As part of my job interview, I had to deliver a job talk in the department, which I based on my first peer-reviewed publication. I remember that I prepared a PowerPoint presentation. When I was discussing a quote in a slide about the female body in the strawberry industry, the professors started to analyze my quote. At UC *Tres Calmecac*, I had seen job talks in the Departments of Anthropology and Chicano Studies where the audience listened with respect. In my job talk, these women were all analyzing my slide. I was surprised at their aggressive attitude during my presentation. I could not believe their disrespectful behavior! It seemed that they had the intellectual capacity, a superior racial-ized faculty, to analyze my own lecture. Ironically, the Universal Studies faculty negated my *facultad*. I could not understand their microaggression, and I felt greatly frustrated.

During the question and answer period, a Chicana scholar asked me, "How would you respond to racial slurs in the classroom?" I was shocked because I expected theoretical or methodological questions. I could not believe the Chicana professor's odd question. I thought that she could have asked a different question to help me shine. As the old Mexican saying goes: *para que la cuña apriete, tiene que ser del mismo palo* (for the wedge to squeeze tied, it has to be from the same wood). I felt that the Chicana professor undermined my *facultad*. I felt betrayed by her! I remember that my hands were sweating profusely and I wanted to cry!

My *facultad* was fully aware that Cal-State was dominated by rich white students whose parents owned multimillion-dollar farms, were donors to Cal-State, hired Mexican immigrants to harvest their crops, employed Mexican nannies in their homes, and Mexican men cared for their multimillion-dollar pure blood Arabian horses. However, I did not think about the racial and class composition of Cal-State since my sister and friends were studying in Cal-State. Later, I understood that as a faculty member I would be expected to coddle rich white students.

As part of the job interview, a white professor took me to dinner in downtown San Luis Obispo. I recalled that this professor was very friendly. They would tell me, "When you come to teach … or you can live in such a place …"They were remarkably friendly and they gave me positive feedback, so I relaxed. Nearing the end of the dinner we were joined by an Asian American professor. During our conversation, this professor revealed that they were doing research with Asian American farmers in Santa Marta and the Central Coast. I had interviewed Japanese American farmers because they had hundreds of Mexican immigrants, Filipino, and Mexican American families working as sharecroppers. Of course, I knew them. I remember going to the bathroom for a few minutes. When I came back, the professors were extremely serious. I thought, "What happened here?" In a few minutes, the conversation shifted from friendly to hostile.

After dinner, the Chair of the Universal Studies Department picked me up from the restaurant. On the way back to my hotel, she said that a professor had invited renowned food justice speaker Michael Pollan to discuss his latest book in Cal-State. According to the Chair, this was against the recommendation of the Dean, and the professor was demoted. I did not ask how a professor could so easily be demoted. I did not dare question the outrageous violation of academic freedom. I realized that agribusiness exerted so much power to prevent Michael Pollan from visiting the public university campus. I was not sure if the Chair of the Universal Studies Department was comparing my social justice work with that of Michael Pollan. I expected the Universal Studies Department to have a social justice orientation and to embrace my non-white performance during the job interview. Nevertheless, I was not surprised when I received the Universal Studies rejection letter. The systemic negation of my *facultad* was difficult to understand. My *facultad* was so heartbroken.

I started to look for another temporary adjunct faculty position at UC *Tres Calmecac* because Maria Antoinette's threat felt real.

I found one course in Feminist Studies and another in the Latin American and Iberian Studies (LAIS) Program. I was immediately assigned to teach general introduction courses. Although I knew that it would be a challenge to teach introductory courses, I accepted. One day, the professor and Chair of the Feminist Studies Department called me into her office. As I opened the door to her office, I was surprised to find the LAIS Director seating next to her. I do not recall the details of the conversation with them, but this meeting was about my negative teaching evaluations. I was flabbergasted because the Chair and the Director ambushed me! I was so angry and I felt humiliated. In Feminist Studies and LAIS, many students were white rich kids, like the ones that blinded my friend and me in our sociology classes, or the ones I would have to coddle and cosset in Cal-State.

While I was working in Feminist Studies, white undergraduate students visited me a lot during office hours. I remember that I had a student who was about 18 years old and loved talking to me in my office hours. In those conversations, I learned that her father was an American diplomat stationed in South Africa. She had lived in so many countries and had attended the best schools. She spoke many languages including Spanish because she had a Spanish-speaking caregiver. I was shocked to find out about her many white upper-class privileges.

I also remember a white student who had a mental health disability. In class, when she disagreed with me, she would tell me outright. She would abruptly interrupt me and I would listen to her disrespectful interventions. When she did not like my speech, she would correct me. She would make fun of me because I spoke English with a Mexican accent. Progressively, I became frustrated by her behavior and asked her to speak to me during office hours. Because I was in a position of authority, she met me in my office. I learned that she had a mental health problem, but I cannot recall the details. I remember thinking that I had many undergraduate students with depression and eating disorders in Feminist Studies. I was puzzled that UCTC was accepting them when instructors did not have the training to help them in class. Nevertheless, I became a compassionate instructor and ignored her disruptions, or racial microaggressions, in class. I mobilized my *facultad*, compassion, affective epistemology, in the classroom while the white institution was threatening my own humanity. (The next section could trigger post-traumatic reactions.)

I never imagined that I would have an existential crisis. After Chicana and Chicano Studies, Universal Studies, Feminist Studies, and LAIS attacked my *facultad*, I was so distraught! I felt so small and so hopeless! One day, I remember driving to the nearest store where I purchased a bottle of cheap, Jose Bold Eagle tequila. I arrived home and opened the bottle with difficulty. I took a sip of tequila. It burned as it went down my throat. Anzaldúa's (1987) concept of Coatlicue, the Goddess of dark and light and ruler of the underworld, was calling my name: Guille, Guille! My body was shaking, and my head was spinning. I ached everywhere as if I was still picking strawberries. I felt that something very precious had been snatched from me. I felt powerless and dispossessed because I lost my precious home in Aztlán!

I took a second shot of Jose Bold Eagle tequila and I began to cry out loud. Salty tears rolled down my brown, round cheeks. I asked myself, what will I do now? I had been slaughtered like the small goats that my dear father purchased for the carnival feast in my hometown. I felt that I was falling into a black hole. I covered my face with my hands and rocked my body slowly. I kept thinking, "How will I survive now?" As I cried out from my soul, I drank more tequila. For the first time in my life, I was very, very drunk! I recalled my *nana doña* Estrella summoning my name when my soul left my body near the river surrounded by venomous snakes. *Doña* Estrella who died decades ago could not light my soul out of Coatlicue's arms. Coatlicue kept dragging me into her darkness. The institution was blinding me and I felt so utterly lost. They denied my culture, history, knowledge, and my *facultad*. In a white Eurocentric institution, I was a fractured neoliberal subject pushed into the zone of nonbeing. The epistemic-ide was brutal! My *facultad*'s energy was dimming. The immigrant Affirmative Action scholar was losing the battleground.

On the second day of my existential crisis, I decided to go to the Chicana and Chicano Studies Department where I found Chicana professor Sofía Infantes Pimentel in her office. I entered and sat on the chair next to her desk. Although her office was small, I felt one million miles away from her. For the first time, I noticed that this beautiful elegant Chicana spoke Spanish with a weird accent. As I sat in front of her, I asked her the reason for her lack of support in the department. She had been copied in the cold termination email. She replied, "It is complicated." Sofía was always friendly towards me, and I considered her a Chicana scholar *camarada* and friend. She utterly failed to support me. I felt that the betrayal pierced my Mexican heart! I took my brown skin, round face with slanted eyes, straight hair, petite female body, broken English, and immigrant poor background as the reason for not succeeding in academia. I became a disgraced Adjunct

Professor, a dishonored Adjunct Professor, and a total academic failure. Years later, I learned that Chicana/o Studies could have retained me in its *facultad*, but they chose to rid the department of Mexican immigrant and critical scholars.

When Chicana and Chicano Studies attacked my *facultad*, I mobilized the *comunalidad* to support me in the struggle to survive as a negated, fractured, Mexican immigrant scholar. One of my friends recommended that I find internal allies to confront Maria Antoinette's visceral attacks in the department. I remember that I spoke to Chicana and Chicano Studies Professor Juan Carlos Perez about Maria Antoinette's plans to dismiss me from teaching in the department. Because Juan Carlos was involved in every social justice demonstration in the campus, I thought that he was a good *camarada* in the department. So, one day, I saw his office door open. I knocked on the door and he replied "Come in". I did not go in, but rather I stood at the door. I spoke to him while he was sitting behind his desk. I explained to him Maria Antoinette's plan with tears in my eyes. After I finished explaining to Juan Carlos the plan to terminate my *facultad*, he replied, "over my dead body". Upon hearing Juan Carlos expressing his solidarity, I felt reassured. In fact, I did not doubt that he would support my position in the department. After all, he was a progressive Chicano scholar who represented the underdogs at UCTC. I thought that I had a progressive social justice advocate, *camarada*, and tenured professor on my side.

I also spoke to Native American Professor Ramona Hernández who was a scholar at UCTC. She had taught courses in the Chicana and Chicano Studies Department and knew many of the professors. When she heard my story, she said, "They have forgotten where they are coming from. [Professors] Carlos Navarro, Constanza Arias, and Enrique Cervantes were civil right activists." I was shocked! These were the most progressive, radical, social justice and civil rights Chicana and Chicano activists. In their elegant suits, they walked in the halls of Chicana and Chicano Studies, but they ignored me and my struggle in the department.

In my struggle to survive in a white institution I met the Social Science Dean a few times. My friend told me to ask him to support my lectureship in the Chicana and Chicano Studies Department. The first time that I met the Dean, he explained that I was a Unit 18 Lecturer subject to the contract between the university and the labor union. The Dean added that the budget to employ lecturers came from the sub-zero account. I did not know nor did I care about the sub-zero account. While the Dean talked, I saw my file on his desk. I had never seen my academic file. I did not even know that such a thing existed.

When I went to see the Dean a second time, he told me that Chicanas like Professor Sofia Navarrete identified as "Indians", yet they were treating "Indians" like me badly. He added that they did not want Indians teaching in Chicana and Chicano Studies. He remarked, "I cannot understand them." The Dean said that he would support me in a different department. So, when a feminist professor offered me a partial lectureship in Feminist Studies, I accepted it. Gutiérrez y Muhs, González, and Flores (2020) discussed the intersectional struggles of women of color in academia. I became demoralized and heartbroken at the racial, gender, class, language, and citizenship violence in the academic world. I realized that the biggest vulnerability was being an adjunct faculty member in academe. In 2017, I left my adjunct position feeling that my *facultad* had been destroyed. My *facultad*, teaching and learning, could not resist white power.

The power of *comunalidad*

Rooted in my experience as a Putleca, or *comunalidad*, I began to reclaim my negated *facultad*. I always admired the energy of my paternal grandfather who learned to read and write in Spanish on his own. In reading his favorite magazine, he became aware of the opportunity to work in the Bracero Program in California. Also, my late father would tell us that education was our inheritance. If we wanted an inheritance, we would receive one. If not, we would suffer the consequences of not taking the opportunity to improve our human condition. My older brother studied at the famous Polytechnic Institute in México City, and my two other brothers completed High School in Santa Marta. These were small, yet powerful, stories of immigrant educational success.

I remember that my beautiful mother considered education a valuable inheritance. Although she never went to the university, she would stress the power of knowledge as a form of freedom from racial, patriarchal, capitalist oppression. She would always tell me, *estudia hija. Estudia porque eso es algo que nadie podrá quitarte nunca* (Daughter, you must study. That is something that nobody will ever take away from you). My mother would encourage all her sons and daughters to educate themselves. I could affirm that she was very successful because all my sisters went to universities. One has a doctoral degree in Clinical Psychology, one has a master's degree in Social Work, and one has a Bachelor's degree in Child Psychology. My sisters had a *facultad* that was put at the service of the immigrant communities. My older son also played an important role supporting me, reading, and editing my publications. Unlike dominant narratives of seeing education as a vehicle for individual socio-economic mobility, for my family education was an exercise in collective freedom. Knowledge became an exercise against racial patriarchal domination.

To rekindle my *facultad*, I relied on the support of my colleagues and friends in academia who were part of a new sense of *comunalidad*. My dearest friend Paula Martínez was finishing her doctoral degree in Sociology when she purchased a guidebook to write academic articles. She invited me to write an article for publication. We followed the guidebook as if it had been written in stone. For several months, we met at a coffee place where we wrote our first peer-review articles. In my case, my Chicano and African American colleagues read my article and gave me valuable feedback. Later, I submitted it to a major scholarly journal. My older son became my professional editor. As a child, I would read stories in English and Spanish to him every night. I would have not survived one day in academia without their support, nor would I publish peer-review articles. With their help, I overcame one of the most powerful technologies of patriarchal and racial exclusion.

I obtained a job as a case worker in a student organization at UC *Tres Calmecac*. After my husband passed away in 2017, I worked helping undergraduate students, faculty and staff, and community members dealing with housing issues and problems in the community. Two years later, I obtained a new job in one of the most important institutions of the university, but they hired me as an office assistant. I have applied to be the director of several research institutions at UCTC to no avail. Today, I work at the bottom of the racial hierarchy. Nonetheless, I have found the opportunity to dedicate weekends and vacation periods to do ethnographic and archival research.

Indeed, I regained my *facultad* as a public intellectual when I decided to do ethnographic and archival research. Although I was dispossessed of my academic employment, I never stopped reading scholarly works. In 2019, I was reading an article published by United Farm Workers [UFW] veteran, Marshall Ganz, that briefly mentioned farm labor cooperatives. I was curious about the labor cooperative in agriculture. I contacted Marshall Ganz asking for references on the labor coops. He did not have any references, but he recommended the UFW archives deposit in the Walter P. Reuther Library at Wayne State University. I was so happy that I could begin a new intellectual project.

I spent months doing archival research on the credit union that farm workers leader César Chávez and the United Farm Worker leadership launched in the 1960s. In the Walter P. Reuther's Library, I found a few samples of *El Malcriado* newspaper advertising the UFW's credit union. Between 1964 and 1970, *El Malcriado* published an average of 20 issues per year and I browsed through more than 100 issues in search of information on the UFW credit union. In the archive, I encountered the Marshall Ganz Papers, and the Arizona Papers at the Walter P. Reuther's Library, which had 24 cases – one-page loan applications with basic information – from men and women farm workers who borrowed microloans from the United Farm Workers credit union. I also found Filipino labor activist Philip Vera Cruz Papers containing the minutes of César Chávez meeting with Puerto Rican Bishop

Antulio Parrilla to talk about cooperatives in Delano. The digital archive had the César Chávez Papers and the Dolores Huerta files on the credit union. Both contained scattered and disorganized financial records. Although I would have loved to do ethnographic research in Santa Marta, I settled for the opportunity to conduct ethnohistorical research using virtual files.

In *El Malcriado* newspaper, I found photographs of Helen Fabela Chávez, César Chávez' wife, who was very important in the management of the credit union. Although many scholars think that Helen did not play an active role in the farm worker movement, she actually managed the collective money. In fact, she was the *matron* of the credit union, but she was always seen through the eyes of her husband César, or in gender stereotypical ways. I also learned that poor Mexican immigrants, Chicanos, and Filipino farm workers would borrow small micro loans varying between $100 and $300, but many did not repay the micro loans. As my research advanced, I was annoyed at finding that the UFW published blacklists of defaulted borrowers. Based on my research on the credit union, I wrote an article and sent it to a peer-review journal. My *facultad*, with deep roots in my sense of transnational *comunalidad*, bloomed like the mango tree in the backyard of my Blue House in Oaxaca.

Conclusion

When I was picking strawberries in my parent's sharecropping plot, I dreamt of having an education to free me from neoliberal, racial, patriarchal, oppression. The educational journey was long, but I was happy with the slow progress. As my *facultad* became more solid, I broke the silence and shamed. After I obtained my doctoral degree, I was happy. For more than a decade, I was subjected to visceral attacks in the nonprofit world and in public Eurocentric educational institutions. Although education became the tool to redress a history of injustice, immigrant women were (and are) denied equal opportunities. For several years, my spirit was broken and I struggled with the failure to survive in academe. The same institution that educated me almost destroyed me. My *facultad* spoke about a broader social project to destroy the advances of the Civil Rights of providing an education to disenfranchise Mexican immigrants in the nation.

I began thinking that I had stories to tell about me and my immigrant community. Thus, I began to do ethnographic and archival research and publishing articles as a public intellectual. I grew more confident in my *facultad*, in my awareness, and intellectual skills. From an exteriority, outside of the system, I found the stability to become a public intellectual.

Conclusion

A Family's Endless Journey illustrates my family and my personal story through the lens of a child's eyes, the border, living labor, and faculty. I grew up in a small town surrounded by the beautiful Sierra Madre mountains located hundreds of kilometers away from Oaxaca City, and México City. As a child growing up in Putla, Oaxaca, my cultural identity was firmly rooted in the *comunalidad* through annual Catholic religious fiestas, rituals like carnival and the parade. My identity also included the sociality of communal foodways when people dressed in their best to celebrate by eating *masa de chivo* and drinking *tepache* together. My sense of belonging as a Putleca, who was born in the Blue House in the *barrio de Arroyos*, was shaped by my brothers, sisters, and friends who played marbles or climbed mango trees with me. My father, who was a well-known person in town, became a respectful *mayordomo* sponsoring the annual feast that accompanies the traditional Catholic carnival ritual to the tune of the local music. I belonged to a place (town, neighborhood, and family) where my identity developed in relation to the pebble streets, rivers, and mountains of an astonishing semi-tropical territory diverse in flora and fauna.

I also acquired political awareness and a sense of social justice in Putla. Although Putla was a seemingly isolated town far away from the centers of power in the country, it was part of local and national political life. Putla was embedded in national anti-guerrilla politics, as my step-grandfather led his cavalry chasing guerrilla fighter Lucio Cabañas. In the mid-1970s, I left my home place to study in the alternative popular preparatory school in México City where my friends and I were protesting the United States imperialist embargo against Cuba. Putla was not an isolated town as global commodities like Coca-Cola or *Kalimán* comic books arrived weekly in town. My grandparents and parents traveled long distances to sell their living labor in the Californian fields.

I belong to a multigenerational Oaxaqueño family whose fragmented emotional lives spanned multiple borderlands and spaces. My grandfather and father joined the United States-Mexican Bracero Program after which my mother's step-brother sponsored his Green Card. A few years later, my mother became a Green Card holder traveling between California and Oaxaca, México, suffering hardships on the road. In the absence of my mother, two Indigenous women cared for me and my siblings, but I experienced emotional trauma yearning for her return to Putla. In the 1970s, while some family members emigrated to Europe, my siblings and I left our homeland in order to study in México City. By the mid-1980s, my Oaxaqueña family settled in Santa Marta and we became part of the "Mexican problem". We were then subjected to the criminal and racist immigration policies of the federal, state, and local governments, but we challenged it by participating in demonstrations. My family inhabited violent spaces spanning the United States and México as some members lived through horrible expressed kidnapping experiences.

My Oaxaqueño family's labor history illustrated major social transformations occurring in the heart of the world's most modern capitalist agrarian economy that exploits poor Mexican immigrant farm workers and their families. In the fields, Guilla's labor revealed the hidden social relations of exploitation and domination while her living labor resisted the material conditions stripping her of a family and homeplace. Guilla, my mother, became a migrant farm worker at the end of the United States-Mexican Bracero Program (1942–1964), and her seven children, Green Card holders, become part of the growing transborder, flexible, non-wage labor force in the strawberry industry whose living labor regained dignity by watching the Dodgers baseball pitcher Fernando Valenzuela. Guilla's daughter's living labor resisted global exploitation and domination of labor by contesting the public displays of stained hands and by listening to her short-wave radio and la Trova Cubana music.

Agribusiness and Mexican *rancheros* built an extremely sophisticated infrastructure to market millions of highly perishable strawberries boxes where cooling plant facilities played an important role. In sharp contrast, Mexican immigrant farm workers, concentrated in poor enclaves, lived in overcrowded conditions, once denounced as the "Mexican problem", in the Santa Marta Valley. In a working-class neighborhood, Guilla, as a retired poor farm worker, cultivates Oaxa-California medical herbs like *hierba santa*, *chayotes*, and *capulines* that bloom in the backyard of her poor home.

Because I began to imagine that I could study at a university in the United States, I slowly built my *facultad* by enrolling at the local city college to learn English as a Second Language, after which I transferred to UC *Tres Calmecac* through the Affirmative Action Program. I worked my way through the school system until I completed my doctoral program with great effort. I was employed in the nonprofit sector for a brief time because I was hired to teach as an adjunct professor in Chicano Studies at UC *Tres Calmecac*. I felt at home in Aztlán, but Chicana and Chicano Studies dismissed me pretty soon, negating my *facultad*. My wounded neoliberal body experienced erasures and negations for a long time. This provoked an existential crisis, and I felt pushed into the zone of nonbeing. I almost died in Coatlicue's arms. It took me a while to overcome the silence and the shame until I finally understood that my intellectual life did not depend on Eurocentric white academic institutions. As a public intellectual, I write my stories from the perspective of a pedagogy of freedom. I claim my right to learn, to do research, and to publish.

Activities and learning objectives

Teachers

Mexican immigration to the United States needs to be explored in-depth from the perspective of lived experiences. This can be done in two ways. In the classroom, you could assign a journal for students to write their ideas, experiences, emotions, awareness, and thoughts related to borders, labor, or education. You could encourage them to write weekly short reflective essays. You also ask them to bring their favorite fruit to class, so that they engage in *comunalidad*. Give them extra credit if they share their memories associated with their particular fruit. The following films, documentaries, and videos can help them visualize and understand the milieu in which Mexican immigrants navigate in a foreign land. Exercise caution as chapters two and four narrate traumatic experiences that could trigger post-traumatic reactions among young readers in the classroom.

Objectives

Students will be able to:

- Research cultural identity in relation to space;
- Discuss how *comunalidad* resists oppression; and
- Apply *comunalidad* to their own experience.

Activity one

This activity focuses on understanding the concept of *comunalidad* and how it produces cultural and political identities. For example, draw a map of my identity in relation to a space, town, neighborhood, and city. Then ask them to identify specific memories (marketplace), sensibilities (sharing), and emotions (affection) in relation to space. For example, have them watch one of the following videos about the carnival in Putla, which are found on YouTube. To help you, use some of the discussion questions below in planning this activity. Although these videos are filmed in Spanish, you can turn on the translations on the Settings button.

Asi es Putla de Guerrero, Oaxaca. (2019). Video. Pepe Velasquez. www.youtube.com/watch?v=BAKMobdIIb4

Plaza de Todo Santos en Putla, Oaxaca. (2024). Video. Pepe Velasquez.
www.youtube.com/watch?v=N2NQ4gZORqE

Caldo de pancita y día de plaza de Putla Villa de Guerrero, Oaxaca. (2023). Video. Ruta Oaxaqueña. www.youtube.com/watch?v=d_9HQAeqLZ0

Discussion questions

What is *comunalidad*?
Are there any symbols of class, race, gender, and/or patriarchal relations?
How did music or poetry shape my political identity?
What are the communal anchors of the homeplace?
Is the marketplace an emotional space?

What were the national and local pressures of political life in Putla? Why was Putla such an ideal place?

Activity two

This activity is about creating an awareness of the historical and political strategies to manage the United States-Mexican border. The following films help students to compare and contrast border crossing stories. Please make sure to give a trigger-warning announcement to students because the films are violent.

Border South (2019). Documentary. Raúl O. Paz Pastrana.

Desierto (2017). Film. Jonás Cuarón.

Discussion questions

What is the meaning of the United States-Mexican border?
How is the border managed? What are the technologies of exclusion?
How is the Green Card a management tool?
Why does the border create fragmented identities or life?
Why is the border an emotional experience?
Why is citizenship a new subjectivity?
Why do immigrants think that citizenship protects our bodies in the nation?

Activity three

This activity serves to illustrate the transnational relationship between home in México and the United States as Mexican immigrants settled throughout rural America.

East of Salinas (2016). Documentary. Jackie Mow.

Ways of Being Home (2020). Film. Cecilia Cornejo.

Discussion questions

What is the role of living labor in agriculture?

Why are there different labor systems?

How many key historical moments do we see in this labor history?

Why is agriculture unethical?

How does *comunalidad* contests domination in agriculture?

Activity four

This activity illustrates the educational and emotional challenges of being rejected in academe. Using the concept of *facultad*, students can write an essay to reflect on their own journey to the university addressing their dreams, hopes, and challenges. In other words, they can apply the concept of *facultad* to their own story or they can write an essay based on one of the following films. Please be aware that I discussed an existential crisis in this chapter.

Stand and Deliver (1988). Film. Ramón Menéndez.

A Million Miles Away. (2023). Film. Alejandra Marquez.

Discussion questions

What is *facultad*?

Why did I say that my *facultad* was negated?

How did I confront white institutions in academe?

What were the challenges for people of color?

Why was an adjunct faculty position a vulnerability?

How did I become a public intellectual?

Afterthoughts

Since the early 1980s, thousands of migrants from Oaxaca, México, crossed the United States-Mexican border. People from Putla and surrounding towns traveled to the northern states of Sonora, Sinaloa, and Baja California. By the end of the decade, Putlecos, many of whom were teachers, crossed the international border and settled in California and New Jersey. Many worked as farm workers, while others found employment in the service sector. In this manner, they supported themselves and their families in Putla. Since the early 2000s, my hometown has changed in many ways.

My parents sent money to build a concrete, three-story, American style home next to their old Blue House in the *barrio de Arroyos*. As *norteños*, or migrants working in California, my father saved money to employ an architect to build a spectacular house that rivaled the houses of the richest families in town. Unlike the old, adobe houses in the neighborhood, a luscious, tropical garden lines the entryway to the house. The gated door guards my father's small Ford truck. The main doors lead to the first floor, dedicated to the greeting of guests and family. The living room is located on the second floor, and has a beautiful, carved dining table and chairs made from an old mango tree. The kitchen and the dining room overlook the town where mango, papaya, and avocado trees provide shade to red bougainvillea and yellow jacaranda trees on hot days. In sharp contrast, the three-story

Californian style house stands next to my parents' old Blue House. Like my parents, Putlecos sent money to build three-story American homes, changing the local landscape. When I visited Putla, I felt like I was in Oaxa-California.

During a recent trip to Putla, I noticed that the economic development of the region is based on the extraction of natural resources. Stones, sand, and water are harvested from mountains and local rivers to meet the demand for paved roads and new concrete homes in Putla and nearby towns. Las Peñitas river, where I spent countless hours swimming as a child, is the private property of a powerful and violent *cacique*. The *cacique* controls an entertainment court, a restaurant, and other amenities on the river's edge. This area is surrounded by barbed-wire *corrals* and armed security guards. When former Mexican president Carlos Salinas de Gortari (1988–1994) modified the 1927 Constitution to allow the selling of Ejido Lands owned by the State, Putla's natural resources were quickly privatized. The privatization of natural resources could not have been done without the sanction of local political bosses. My friends and I quietly criticize the privatization of the public domain, fearing repercussions from the *cacique*.

Upon arriving at the bus terminal in Putla, I was surprised to see dozens of young men, women, and children lining the sidewalks of the highway. My friends explained they were "Central Americans" who began to arrive in Putla over the last two years. I heard many people speaking Spanish with Venezuelan and Colombian accents. I also heard other non-Spanish languages. Buses loaded with "Central Americans" arrive in my hometown every day. While they wait for the next bus to go to México City or Oaxaca City, they stay on the streets adjacent to the bus terminal, in nearby hotels, and in the main plaza of the town.

When I visited my friends in their homes, I heard harrowing stories. One of my friends told of a young couple traveling with a two-year-old. The child was running a high fever and, while the pharmacy had medication, they had no way to cover or protect the child at night and during the cold mornings. My friend also said that a young woman left her little girl in the care of a local woman. She could no longer protect her child in the long, inhospitable, and dangerous trek to the United States, and opted to leave her in Putla. In the main plaza, I saw pregnant women, women with children, and nuclear families waiting for the bus. I could not avoid feeling a deep sense of sadness thinking about the reasons for which they left their homes, towns, and families. Putla is no longer the small town that I left behind forty years ago. Like Tijuana, Putla is now a border town.

Glossary of Spanish words

agua fresca	sweet water with fruit
aguardiente	sugarcane local alcoholic beverage
arrieros	vendors herding mules from town-to-town
auxilio	help
Aztlán	Chicano homeland
barrio	neighborhood
borracha	drunkard
buchicata	tropical plant
caballito	a term that refers to a wheelbarrow
cabecera de municipio	roughly translated as county seat
Calmecac	pre-Hispanic university among the Aztecs.
camarada	comrade
cantinas	bars
caña	sugarcane
capulines	native fruit similar to cherries
careo	two contradictory versions of an event
cargo	communal obligation

carrilla	pushed the crew
chapulines	grasshoppers
chayotes	a pre-Hispanic fruit belonging to the squash family
cazuela de barro	clay pot
chilacayote	homemade sweet drink from a squash-like fruit
chile	chili
chingadera	roughly translated as the "shitty thing"
chiso	gift for buying the merchandise
chupamirtos	hummingbirds
comandante	commander
compadre	person becomes a co-parent after a religious ritual
corral	barbed-wire fence
corrido	ballad
coyote	term that refers to a smuggler
culers	Spanish-English term to refer to cooling-shipping centers
cunis	turkey-like structure
curandera	folk healer
Doña	female title showing respect to an older person
escardando	hoeing

garita	Border inspection booth
gatas	term used to pejoratively refer to maids
gelatina de pata	treat made from cow hooves
granadas	fruit similar to pomegranate
guanavos	fruit similar to *chirimoya*
huajes	edible vines with seeds
huipiles	traditional handwoven wool dresses
madrina	godmother
masa de chivo	goat's soup
mascaritas	masked dancers
mayordomo	man communally obligated to feed the dancers
mercado	marketplace
mole	traditional spicy thick soup
nana	female caregiver
norteño	migrant living and working in the United States
ollas de barro	clay pots
palomas	doves
pan de llema	bread with egg's yolk
pan de muerto	Day of the Dead bread
papaloquelites	A native edible plant
patria	country

perro	dog
peso	national currency
pierna de vieja	native edible plant
planchada	term that literally means ironing
presidencia municipal	similar to a local city council
pollito	chick
pozole	traditional spicy corn soup
pueblos Indígenas	autochthonous towns
quinceañera	coming-of-age ritual to celebrate the sweet 15 birthday anniversary
rancheros	growers
revistas de historietas	comic books
secuestro	kidnapping
semitas	bread with sesame seeds on it
susto	experience of extreme fright when the soul leaves the body
tamal	traditional staple food wrapped in banana leave
tepache	fermented corn alcoholic drink
terlenka	polyester fabric
tianguis	pre-Hispanic place of exchange and knowledge
tilichis	costume

torito	wooden structure covered with cow skin that resembles a cow
totopos con frijol y queso	bean and cheese crispy tortillas
usos y costumbres	traditional rights and costumes
viejo	old man
Virgen de Natividad	patron saint
yerba santa	edible plant

References

Anzaldúa, G. (1987). *Borderlands/La Frontera: The New Mestiza*. San Francisco: aunt lute books.

Bardacke, F. (2012). *Trampling Out the Vintage: Cesar Chavez and the Two Souls of the United Farm Workers*. Verso.

Bautista, R. (2014). *La descolonización de la política: Introducción a una política comunitaria*. La Paz, Bolivia: Agruco/Plural Editores.

Córdoba, M. E. and de la Calle, C. (2016). La Alteridad desde la perspectiva de la Transmodernidad de Enrique Dussel. *Revista Latinoamericana de Ciencias Sociales*, 14(2), pp. 1001–1015.

de Leon, J. (2015). *The Land of Open Graves: Living and Dying on the Migrant Trail*. Berkeley: University of California Press.

Dussel, E. D. (2016). *14 Tesis de ética: hacia la esencia del pensamiento crítico*. Madrid, Spain: Editorial Trotta, S. A.

Givens, J. R. (2021). *Fugitive Pedagogy: Carter G. Woodson and the Art of Black Teaching*. Cambridge, Massachusetts: Harvard University Press.

Grimes, K. M. (1998). *Crossing Borders: Changing Social Identities in Southern Mexico*. Arizona: University of Arizona Press.

Gutiérrez y Muhs, G., González, C. M., and Flores Niemann, Y. eds. (2020). *Presumed Incompetent II: The Intersections of Race and Class for Women in Academia*. Utah: Utah State University Press.

Holmes, S. (2013). *Fresh Fruit, Broken Bodies: Migrant Farm Workers in the United States*. Berkeley: University of California Press.

Khosravi, S. (2010). *"Illegal" Traveller: An Autoethnography of Borders*. London: Palgrave Macmillan Press.

Khosravi, S. (2018). A Fragmented Diaspora. *Nordic Journal of Migration Research*, 8(2), pp. 73–81.

Maldonado Alvarado, B. (2015). Perspectivas de la comunalidad de los pueblos indígenas de Oaxaca. *Bajo el Volcán*, 15(23), septiembre 2015–febrero 2016, pp. 151–169.

Martínez Luna, J. (2010). Eso que llaman comunalidad. Colección díalogos, Oaxaca.

Martínez Luna, J. (2022). Saberse naturaleza para razonar y contruir conocimiento/We Recognize Ourselves as Part of Nature to Reason and to Build Knowledge. *Utopía y praxis Latinoamericana*, 27(98), pp. 1–10.

Marx, K. (1961 ed.). *Capital Vol. 1*. Trans. S. Moore and E. Aveling. Ed. F. Engels. Moscow: Foreign Languages Publishing House.

Mignolo, W. D. (2021). Ayni and Netilitztli: The Reconstitutions of the Destituted. *Cultural Dynamics*, 33(3), pp. 246–252.

Mills, F. B. (2018). *Enrique Dussel's Ethics of Liberation: An Introduction*. Cham: Springer International Publishing.

Munoz, R. (2011). Big Problems in Santa Marta. *Santa Marta Times*. Available at: www.santamariatimes.com/news/opinion/mail bag/big-problems-in-santa-maria/article_e702332e-88db-11e0-9015-001cc4c002e0.html [Accessed April 11, 2022].

Nicolas, B. (2021). "Soy de Zoochina": Transborder *comunalidad*: Practices among Adult Children of Indigenous Migrants. *Latino Studies*, 19, pp. 47–69.

Palerm, J. V. and Urquiola, J. (1993). A Binational System of Agricultural Production: The Case of the Mexican Bajio and California. In: D. G. Aldrich, Jr. and L. Meyer, eds., *Mexico and the United States: Neighbors in Crisis*. California: The Borgo Press, pp. 311–368.

Pawel, M. (2006). Farmworkers Reap Little as Union Strays from Its Roots. *Los Angeles Times*. Available at: www.latimes.com/local/la-me-ufw8jan08-story.html [Accessed April 30, 2022].

Sánchez-Antonio, J. C. (2021). Genealogía de la comunalidad indígena: Descolonialidad, transmodernidad y diálogos inter-civilizatorios. *Latin American Research Review*, 56(3), pp. 696–710.

Wells, M. (1996). *Strawberry Fields: Politics, Class, and Work in California Agriculture*. Ithaca: Cornell University Press.

Wolf, E. (1957). Closed-Corporate Peasant Communities of Mesoamerica and Central Java. *Southwestern Journal of Anthropology*, 12, pp. 1–18.

Index